*Finding
Balance*

EDITED BY SHEILA JONES

Finding
Balance
from the inside out

DPI

DISCIPLESHIP
PUBLICATIONS
INTERNATIONAL

Finding Balance
©2002 by Discipleship Publications International
2 Sterling Rd., Billerica, Mass., 01862-2595

Printed in the United States of America

ISBN: 1-57782-179-3

Cover and interior design: Jennifer Matienzo

Contents

Balance Survey

1. How would you describe a balanced life?

2. What is your greatest challenge in balancing your life?

3. What have you learned about saying no?

4. How do you find time to be in God's word and prayer?

5. In what ways do you want to grow in having a better balance?

6. What is the key (or what are the keys) to having a balanced life?

7. Are you tempted to feel guilty about the choices that you make? If so, how do you deal with that guilt?

8. How do you allow other people to help you maintain balance?

9. What are the signs you look for to know that your life is getting out of balance?

10. Do you have any specific, practical tips for maintaining order in life? (examples: how you clean, how you keep up with groceries, meals, laundry)

Preface

I saw a birthday card the other day that spoke of the balanced life. On the outside it said,

On your birthday may you find perfect balance.

Then on the inside was a picture of a yoga master in a traditional position of balance...sitting with folded legs, both arms bent and extended, palms facing upward. Underneath it said,

One bite of cake, one bite of ice cream, one bite of cake, one bite of ice cream...

If only finding balance in life were that easy—and that delicious. But find it we must (as Yoda would say). With the help of God and his word, and with the help of other faithful women, find it we will. This is what *Finding Balance* is all about.

To prepare for this book, I put my ear to the ground. I wanted to hear the rumblings and grumblings, the fears and the tears, the prayers and the cares, the hopes and the mopes of Christian women. I wanted to produce a book that would be real and helpful and hopeful. To surface some answers, I circulated the survey on the previous page.

Here are some responses to the first two questions.

How would you describe a balanced life?

A balanced life, to me, is a life that is attractive to others and draws others in. It [is] a life that has the "usual" issues (bills, relationships,

7

cars, groceries, homes, family, time constraints, battles of the heart, etc.), but the noticeable difference is in the way that they are handled—with grace, patience and understanding.

—Sharon

A balanced woman is someone who lives out the example that the Proverbs 31 woman set for us. She seemed so in tune with all she needed to do, and yet, in the passage the writer doesn't indicate any negative aspects of how she dealt with the many plates she was spinning. You do hear that her husband praised her, that she gave to others selflessly and that she was outward-focused even though she was a busy woman.

—Carol Ann

A balanced life means God always first, [then] marriage, children, career, in that order! And praying to Jesus for the strength to do it all for his glory! As far as I can see, all of my answers will be God-centered because he's the only way anything works!

—Nancy

Feeling happy and secure about my relationship with God and being able to manage my life (career, family, marriage, work, ministry) without being overly stressed and anxious. Enjoying the life of being a disciple of Jesus, despite having a very busy and hectic schedule.

—Teresa

For me, a balanced life meets the needs of all life's priorities: relationship with God, [church], family, friends, etc., without compromising one over another.

—Jill

What is your greatest challenge in balancing your life?

It has always been time. There doesn't seem to be enough [time] in some days to get things accomplished. People in our lives demand time from us—our employers, our families, our friends. I love my job and my family and my friends and want to spend time with all. When I don't get to do what I want, or when I do it all, then I get frustrated and tired and short-tempered.

—Kathryn

My greatest challenge in balancing my life is determining the priorities. When should I be staying up late to serve, when should I be getting rest to make sure I am my best for God at my job and in my ministry, etc.?

—Sharon

My greatest challenge in balancing my life is finding enough time to devote to each relationship to keep the closeness needed.

—Gail

Balancing where to put my attention and effort. Time is a challenge, but effort is harder. There are so many needs: my own spirituality, my daughter, my dating relationship, the lost. I feel pulled in so many opposing directions at times I just want to shut down. It's hard to discern what needs your attention and nurturing. My nature is to help everyone and take care of everything. Where's the balance?

—Christine

What is your greatest challenge to finding balance in your life? Did you see yourself in the honest responses above? I know I did!

It is my prayer, and the prayer of the other authors of this book, that we can help you find the balance in life that Jesus came to bring us. It is our hope that you, along with us, can live the abundant life that God created us to have.

Overwhelm Land

This is a book that is sorely needed by many women I talk with. They say things like, "How can I do it all?" or "I am overwhelmed by life" or "There is too much to do, and I'll never get it all done!" For all you out there wandering in Overwhelm Land, this book is for you!

The authors have proven themselves to be women of balance as they do their tightrope walk of life. And remember, this doesn't mean they walk perfectly; they always walk with a net! They realize that they need God, his word and his people to help them maintain their balance for a lifetime.

In preparation for writing her chapter, many of the writers interviewed women who are great examples of finding balance in their different life situations: single, single mom, working mom, mom of young children, mom of teenage children, mom of special needs children, empty nester and many more. The goal was to get an overall view of daily life, daily struggles, daily victories and daily strategies. In each chapter you will hear from these women both directly (as they are quoted) and indirectly (as they gave input).

Balance Groups

The book is formatted to be easily used in a small group setting. In order to evaluate our lives and to make new commitments to achieving balance, we need other women to give us support, correction, encouragement and feedback. The members of a "Balance Group" can be each other's trainers, mentors and cheerleaders. If you are interested in starting a Balance Group, see the suggestions on page 183.

Certainly, you can read and apply this book outside of a group setting, but we, the editor and authors, encourage you to pull in at least one woman who will attempt this walk with you.

At the end of each chapter, you will find two pages of questions and comments to help you and your group (if you elect to have one) to make personal application of the material.

∽∾

As we together search and together find the abundant, balanced life to which God has called us, to this all-loving, all-patient and totally balanced God be the glory.

—Sheila Jones
Associate Editor
Discipleship Publications International

Group Session One

Questions

1. After reading the preface, take some time to write out your own answers to the Balance Survey on page 6.

2. What aspect of balance is most difficult for you?

Action Item

- Talk with several other people about their perspective on living a balanced life. Ask some of the questions above to help you understand the thoughts and struggles of other women in your life.

Meeting Time

1. Share some of your survey answers with your Balance Group (or balance partner).

2. Read aloud Other Helps, "Suggestions for Balance Groups."

3. Discuss the reading. Do you see yourself and your friends in the scenario given? Explain.

4. Each person makes a verbal commitment to the group to

   a. meet consistently at the time set by the group

   b. read the next chapter, answer the questions, and do the action items before coming to the next meeting

   c. share honestly and openly about victories and struggles

   d. encourage and instruct each other as you all seek to live a life pleasing to God

5. Commit to read chapter 1, "The Balanced Life," answer the questions, and do the action items before coming to the next meeting.

6. Pray together.

Remember to be each other's trainers,
mentors and cheerleaders as you work on the
same things at the same time.

chapter 1
The Balanced Life

1

Sheila Jones
Boston, USA

*I*t seems that everybody and their dogs are writing books on balance these days. (My dog has read several to date…see page 206 to check out her progress.) Perhaps this is such a hot topic because women are busier than ever and have the technology to help them be even busier. Now instead of being "out of radio contact" when driving in our cars, we are reachable by cell phones that play "Yankee Doodle Dandy" and send faxes and e-mails. Since we have no more unreachable places of solitude, we are constantly being bombarded with something to think, something to do, somewhere to go, someone to talk to. Where in all this modern mobility do we slow down enough to catch our collective breath and take stock of our lives and their direction?

We live our lives much like an artist in a high-wire act, seeking the place of perfect balance. Where do we find that place of balance, that center of gravity that will allow us to cross the challenging high wire of life? Some seek their spiritual equilibrium through meditation, New Age teachings, crystals, exercise or even hobbies. As disciples, we seek our spiritual equilibrium through Jesus of Nazareth—the only person who ever lived a perfectly balanced life.

My guess is that few of us have been trained in the fine art of *funambulism*. Just in case this word is unfamiliar to some of us, here

17

is a definition: "tightrope walking: from the Latin *funis* (rope) and *ambulare* (walk)." As we make the comparison of living the Christian life to performing a daring high-wire act, we will discover some helpful principles:

1. Find your center of gravity
2. Have a focal point
3. Be aware of the variables
4. Be grateful for the net

Find Your Center of Gravity

You may have noticed that a high-wire walker usually uses a long pole to help her maintain her balance. In fact, this pole can be as long as thirty-nine feet and can weigh as much as thirty-one pounds. There is a reason for taking a pole with her when she is sixty feet above the ground on a half-inch metal wire—she certainly wouldn't take something extraneous or distracting while ambling across space. She needs the pole because it adds weight, which shifts her center of gravity. You may remember from science class that the center of gravity is the point at which the mass of the object is centered, the balancing point. So having the pole enables the walker to lower her center of gravity, which makes balancing on the thin wire much more like walking on the ground. In fact, if the high-wire walker carries enough weight on the ends of her pole, she can shift her center of gravity to below her. Then walking on the high wire requires "no more sense of balance than...hanging from the wire."[1]

---

[1] Information received from the Web: "Circus High Wire" Newton's Apple is a production of KTCA Twin Cities Public Television. Made possible by a grant from 3M. Educational materials developed with the National Science Teachers Association.

The correct stance on the wire is an upright, straight-backed stance. Then with this stance, the walker leans into the pole, allowing it to maintain her balance. Basically, she does not trust her own ability to balance without the pole because her natural center of gravity will cause her body to start rotating about an axis…that is, fall.

As Christians, the word of God is our balancing pole. It keeps us moving forward with focus and direction. It keeps us from falling to our spiritual death. It helps us find our center of spiritual gravity and keep our balance as we go about our daily life walk:

> I seek you with all my heart;
>   do not let me stray from your commands.
> I have hidden your word in my heart
>   that I might not sin against you. (Psalm 119:10–11)

Have a Focal Point

In an interview with *Decision* magazine, Tino Wallenda of the famous Flying Wallendas, shared what he learned from his grandfather:

> When I was seven years old, my grandfather, Karl Wallenda, put me on a wire two feet off the ground. He taught me all the elementary skills: how to hold my body so that I remained stiff and rigid; how to place my feet on the wire with my big toe on the wire and my heel to the inside; how to hold the pole with my elbows close to my body. But the most important thing that my grandfather taught me was that I needed to focus my attention on a point at the other end of the wire. I need a point to concentrate on to keep me balanced.[2]

The writer of Hebrews understood this concept of fixing our eyes on a certain point in order to keep our balance in life:

---

[2] Tino Wallenda, *Decision,* April 1999.

> Let us fix our eyes on Jesus, the author and perfecter of
> our faith, who for the joy set before him endured the cross,
> scorning its shame, and sat down at the right hand of the
> throne of God. (Hebrews 12:2)

Tino was taught not to look at his feet or his audience or the ceiling of the circus tent. Rather, he fixed his eyes on a point to give him perspective—then he gave himself to his walk.

Jesus truly is our perspective point. The reason is not only that he is the Son of God (reason enough!), but that he walked through this life and never once lost his balance. He never once got distracted or forgot what he was doing. He lived for thirty-three years and never sinned—not even once!

Life muscled in on him too. He did not live a solitary existence in a monastery; he had continual choices as to how he apportioned his twenty-four hours among people, just as we do. The One who *was*, before time came into being, willingly subjected himself to the earthly constriction of time. And within that constriction, he prayed to his God daily and stayed connected to him every moment. His every impulse was guided by his Father (John 8:28–29). In chapter 2 we will spend some time looking at the balance he found in life as he established himself as our perspective point.

Do you want to live a balanced life? I sure do! Then we need to keep our eyes on Jesus, "the author and perfecter of our faith."

Be Aware of the Variables

High-wire walkers have to be aware of the variables, especially the weather. Philippe Petit, who more than twenty-five years ago walked a wire that he had secretly stretched between the then existent World

Trade Center towers, says that the "wind is the wire walker's night-mare."[3] A wise walker always considers his variables when planning and executing a walk.

As disciples of Jesus, we too must consider our variables as we endeavor to live a balanced life. We are all at different stages with different variables: full-time jobs, aging bodies, health challenges, small children, dependent parents, teenagers, ministry responsibilities, etc. Each of us needs to

1. be aware of the variables that make up our lives...and how they interact with each other;

2. know which combination of those variables can cause us to get off balance; and

3. know how to get a plan for dealing with our unique variables.

There are no "cookie cutter" schedules. Each woman must work out not only her own salvation, but also her own schedule and time allotments.

Be Grateful for the Net

> [God's grace] teaches us to say "No" to ungodliness and worldly passions, and to live self-controlled, upright and godly lives in this present age. (Titus 2:12)

Karl Wallenda taught his grandson Tino how to walk the high wire. But he was unable to fully be his safety net if he fell. The wonder of God's grace is that it teaches us how to walk the life of a Christian, but it also catches us when we fall. It is the most secure net: when we fall, it catches us—every time—and folds us in God's perfect love. In fact, it is only because of God's grace that we are even on the wire at all.

---

[3] Calvin Tomkins, "The Man Who Walks on Air," *The New Yorker,* 5 April 1999: 80–87.

God's grace teaches us to be focused on living a righteous life and to also be focused on the only One who ever lived one. It teaches us to hold on to the Scriptures to maintain our balance and not to trust in ourselves. It speaks to all our life situations and instructs us in knowing when to pull out all the stops and when to set righteous boundaries. But as we fail in any of these areas, every day, it graciously catches us and bounces us back into life, free to live it to the full.

From Fellow Funambulists

I asked several exemplary spiritual women in the Boston area to share with me their perspectives on balance:

• *Rose (school teacher/church family-group leader/young children)*

"As a disciple, a balanced life is one centered around Christ. This almost doesn't seem like balance, to have any one thing permeate all aspects of your life, but I have experienced that centering my life around Jesus is the only way to achieve balance. I believe this is because Jesus and God help us to be balanced.

"My own character is my greatest challenge to achieving balance. I can be very focused and this can be good and bad. When I become too focused on one thing, I sometimes neglect other things. For example, I can neglect my family's needs due to pressing schoolwork and/or ministry needs. I think my kids will always be there, but that time is sometimes lost forever and cannot be made up, especially if I were to consistently handle things this way.

"I have learned that I must say no and not feel bad about it because it's for my best spiritually and for the good of my family that I not take on more than I can handle. It is hard to disappoint others, but I feel great about wanting to help, even if I can't. I feel bad when my heart is not wanting to help. If I don't say no, I sometimes feel resentful and angry with myself for being "bullied" and not standing up for what I think is best to do. This is worse than feeling that I want to help but really can't."

- ## Gail (homemaker/elder's wife/children out of the nest)

"A balanced life to me would be one where I am loving God with all my heart first and foremost, and then loving my husband with all my heart, then my kids, and then other people. A balanced life to me would look like this: I would have a close emotional relationship with God through spending time with him in prayer and the Bible. I would have a close emotional relationship with my husband, kids and others by spending great time with them, in open communication, back and forth. I wouldn't be stressed or worried, but trusting, patient and giving.

"My greatest challenge in balancing my life is finding enough time to devote to each relationship to keep the closeness needed."

- ## Diana (accountant/single mom/preschool child)

"A balanced life is one where each part of your life gets a fair share of nurturing and attention.

"I've realized that I alone cannot do everything that comes my way. I only have two arms, two legs, one mind, and I can only be in one place at one time. So how does the rest get accomplished? I had to learn to surrender everything to God in prayer. When I neglect my time with God, I'm not able to surrender and let God take care of things for me. My challenge at times is to stop everything and have that time with God."

• *Vickie (copy editor/teen leader/single)*

"I used to think it meant a 'problem free' life. However, I realize this won't exist until heaven. Therefore the balanced life, to me, is a life of unwavering trust and fruitful labor—not dependent on circumstances or people's approval. Balance means being so tight with God that I am confidently and freely becoming the best 'me' that I can—for God's glory. To see what balance looks like, I look to Jesus.

"True, spiritual balance requires, among other things, courage and faith. These are currently my biggest challenges. (I've learned that I have different challenges with balance during different phases of my life.)

"I learned that life won't end if I say no to something or somebody! I can say no, and it is okay. The irony of saying no is that someone else will get the opportunity to fill the need, and this is a good thing. So while I have a victory saying no, I could help someone else have a victory saying yes. I've had various people actually thank me for giving them the chance to use a hidden talent—simply because I had to pass. Also, I've learned it is important to say no with a grateful, humble heart and a sincere tone.

"I need to be radical in putting God first. Matthew 6:33 is as true today as it was on my baptism day. In seeking balance as a single woman, I see that I have the freedom and flexibility to pursue God like crazy! I am sad when I think of the joy I've wasted by not approaching balance in this way. When I focus on finishing lists and planning activities, I am not fulfilled. When I focus on loving God and loving others, I am refreshed, excited, thrilled to be alive!

"Key one to living a balanced life is Jesus. Key two is Jesus. Key three is Jesus. I am more and more impressed with Jesus' life, words, heart. I constantly beg God for him to show me how I can be like Jesus today—as a single woman, working in twenty-first century America."

It is encouraging to know that God never asks of any of us more than he will, through his spirit, enable us to do. These four women are daily learning this truth as they seek first his kingdom. Jesus says that if we do seek first his kingdom, all the other things we need will be given to us as well. One of the things we desperately need is balance in life. Is it any surprise that in seeking first his kingdom, we are also given the peace of a balanced life?

Total Commitment

As you continue your pursuit of balance in your life, please remember that it is never God's will for you to leave out any aspect that he has called you to. Seeking balance never means lessening our commitment to God or his commands. For example, in order to serve our husbands, we do not give up sharing our faith with others. In order to meet needs in the church, we do not neglect our children. In order to study our Bibles, we do not come in late to work. Seeking balance should never mean taking a break from doing God's will. It simply means finding peace while being faithful in all the responsibilities God has called us to; being motivated by God's love and not self-engendered guilt; and following the example of Jesus:

> Whoever claims to live in him must walk as Jesus did.
> (1 John 2:6)

The truth is that we will never live a balanced life unless we surrender to Jesus and his will. We might live an organized life, but not a balanced life. The two are very different...from the inside out.

৩৹৶

In the popular children's book *Mirette on the High Wire,* a famous high-wire performer comes to stay at Mirette's mother's boarding house. Mirette discovers him walking on the wire he has set up in the backyard, and she longs to walk the wire just like he does:

> Her feet tingled, as if they wanted to jump up on the wire beside Bellini.
> He told her, "Once you start, your feet are never happy again on the ground."
> Her reply was, "Oh please teach me! My feet are already unhappy on the ground."[4]

We can say to Jesus, the Master, the only One who walked with perfect balance through life, "Please teach us. Our feet are unhappy on the ground. We want to walk life as you walked it. And we want to walk it all the way into heaven."

4 Emily Arnold McCully, *Mirette on the High Wire* (New York: G. P. Putnam's Sons, 1992).

Group Session Two

Questions

1. After reading chapter 1, "The Balanced Life," write down the aspect of the high-wire walking analogy that was the most meaningful to you. Why?

2. Write out what you want to learn and how you want to change from reading this book and working together with your Balance Group.

3. Reread the comments of each of the four women who gave their perspective on balance. Which one do you most relate to and why?

Action Items

• After prayer and study, decide on a scripture that is going to be your theme scripture as you learn more about what it means to live a balanced life.

• Memorize that scripture and display it in a highly visible place.

Meeting Time

1. Share with each other your answers to each of the above questions.

2. Share your theme scripture and why you chose it.

3. Read aloud the paragraph under the heading "Total Commitment" on page 25. Share with the group what you want your motivation to be as you seek to live a balanced life.

4. Commit to read chapter 2, "Jesus Defines Balance," answer the questions, and do the action item before coming to the next meeting.

5. Pray together.

Remember to say to Jesus, the Master, the only One who walked with perfect balance through life, "Please teach me. My feet are unhappy on the ground. I want to walk life as you walked it. And I want to walk it all the way into heaven."

chapter 2
Jesus Defines Balance

2

Tammy Fleming
Los Angeles, USA

Let us fix our eyes on Jesus....

Hebrews 12:2

This is how we know we are in him: Whoever claims to live
in him must walk as Jesus did.

1 John 2:5–6

"Follow me."

Luke 9:59

*E*very morning at the kitchen table, in the shortly-after-dawn still-
ness before the kids wake up, I pore over the book of Luke. I'm
straining to catch every move Jesus makes, trying to imagine myself
following step by step, right behind him. In chapter 3, I'm thrilled as
Jesus prays after his baptism and God's own voice is heard from heav-
en: "This is my Son, whom I love...." Yes, I can imagine this!

Chapter 4, verse 1: Jesus, full of the Holy Spirit, led by the Spirit.
Yes, this is what I want for my life; this is what I need! But wait—he
"was led by the Spirit in the desert, where for forty days he was tempted by the devil. He ate nothing during those days, and at the end of
them he was hungry." Already, right there, Jesus' ministry has hardly

even begun, and I'm stopped dead in my tracks. A forty-day fast? I'm irritable and weak after missing one meal! I understand trials and tests will come, but to face Satan himself? Right away? When he is weak and irritable? With nobody else around?

Balance, I remind myself, *we're seeking balance here. Let's see what's next.*

I stumble along after Jesus through the pages of Luke. With the quest for balance in mind, what perplexes me is the apparent lack of any of it in the life of our Lord—as I am defining it anyway. He infuriates the people of a Galilean synagogue so much that they drive him out of town and want to throw him off a cliff. After dark, when he is a guest at Simon's house, the townspeople bring all the sick people to him, and even those possessed by demons. The demons shout, "You are the Son of God!" when they come out. *What must the neighbors be thinking?* I muse. He doesn't seem to sleep much, as he goes out to pray at daybreak right after this, and on another occasion stays out all night praying, and on yet another occasion is so exhausted by the onset of evening that he falls asleep on the deck of a boat during a violent storm! Relentless crowds follow him, almost crushing him, wanting to be taught, to be fed, to be healed. Lepers and paralytics fall in front of him, demanding his immediate attention. He warns those who pledge allegiance to him that though foxes and birds have a home and a place to rest, "the Son of Man has no place to lay his head."

No wonder we struggle, sometimes, as women, to accept Jesus' tightrope walk through life as our model. What kind of reference point is this? A single man, in the prime of his life, presumably in good health, with no children to raise and no secular job to balance as he goes around making disciples—how can I relate to him?

But we know his life was perfectly balanced because he was perfect. He always had the right perspective. He never gave in to serving himself. He always did what the Father wanted him to do—each day, each hour, each moment. That is a perfectly balanced life.

Even though we realize that Jesus did have perfect balance in his response to God's will, we must acknowledge that it is a struggle to relate to Jesus. Our natural tendency is to try to achieve balance in our lives based on culturally accepted human values instead of on spiritual values. Crowds of many thousands who listened to his teaching on hillsides in Galilee had the same natural tendency. Many heard his words but never understood the meaning of his words. Yet every word he spoke was true. Every parable he taught hit the center of the target. His teaching was designed to lead people to the very heart of God: the place of perfect balance. Many were so offended that they turned away…and missed the mark of pleasing God.

Our hearts are tested when we attempt to follow the Jesus of Scripture, just as were the hearts of our sisters two millennia ago who followed the Word of God in the flesh.

Balance: The True Standard

I believe that we get overwhelmed sometimes under the pressure of striving for a balanced life because we are still worldly (1 Corinthians 3:1). Often, our idea of balance is not the true, Biblical definition, nor does it stem from spiritual conviction. Sometimes we are striving for a balance between elements of our lives based on a subjective standard that is our own or that of our culture or some other human perspective. Unless we change our perspective, true balance will elude us, leaving us (1) harried by trying to do it all on our own power or (2) protecting and "saving" ourselves in worldly ways.

A balance can be defined as "an instrument for weighing, or a means of judging or deciding." How did Jesus decide his priorities or judge his effectiveness or weigh the worth of his accomplishments day by day? The standard he used is evident in his prayer, conversation and teaching:

> "For I have come down from heaven not to do my will but to do the will of him who sent me." (Luke 6:38)

> Then he said to them all: "If anyone would come after me, he must deny himself and take up his cross daily and follow me. For whoever wants to save his life will lose it, but whoever loses his life for me will save it. What good is it for a man to gain the whole world, and yet lose or forfeit his very self?" (Luke 9:23–25)

> If someone forces you to go one mile, go with him two miles. Give to the one who asks you, and do not turn away from the one who wants to borrow from you. (Matthew 5:41)

> He went away a second time and prayed, "My Father, if it is not possible for this cup to be taken away unless I drink it, may your will be done." (Matthew 26:42)

Jesus' standard for balance in his life weighed everything based on God's will for him and the various needs of other people. His measuring scales did not seem to be calibrated according to what his own personal desires were! In Matthew 14:1–11, Jesus experienced what we would probably all judge as a very tough day: his cousin, whom he respected as a great prophet of God, was brutally murdered. Hearing this, he took his disciples away to a private place, presumably to mourn, but the crowds following him found out and intruded on this time. However, he had compassion on them and welcomed them, healing all who needed healing. At the end of that difficult day, when it seemed that his closest disciples had had enough, they asked Jesus to send the crowds away. Undeterred, Jesus continued to give to the multitudes and miraculously provided a meal for five thousand men.

Yet at other times, Jesus left the crowds behind (Mark 4:36) and dismissed them (Matthew 14:22). He did not always do what people wanted him to do. He was compassionate and met people's needs, but he was governed neither by their desires nor his own desires. He was governed by God's desires for him at any given time and in any given place.

Our standard for balance in our lives—the impulse we follow to set priorities—is often based on the way we feel. Knowing how we feel in response to whatever is going on in our lives is critically important. Romans 12:3 teaches that we need to have a sober estimate of ourselves or to not think we're doing better than we actually are—emotionally or otherwise. But ignoring our personal feelings or felt needs is not what Jesus meant by self denial or else he could never have expected us to love our neighbors as ourselves (Matthew 22:39). However, seeking balance based on emotional impulses is not going to lead to a spiritually steady promenade across the tightrope.

So, what do we do when we feel overwhelmed, when we're living in Overwhelm Land? Did Jesus ever suffer that sorry state? Certainly he must have, as he was "tempted in every way, just as we are" (Hebrews 4:15).

The secret to his maintaining balance? Jesus often withdrew to lonely places and prayed (Luke 5:15). I believe frequent prayer sustained him, as well as deep convictions based on God's word, such as the principle in 1 Corinthians 10:13: God will not let you be tempted beyond what you can bear. We are worldly, not spiritual, when we think that the problem with our balance or the reason we are overwhelmed lies in current situations such as the number of needs we're being asked to meet (too many!) or the kinds of tasks we're being asked to do (too hard!) or the inappropriate timing of it all (too soon!). In fact, if not even a sparrow falls to the ground apart from the will of our Father (Matthew 10:29), then God is always in control. Jeremiah 17:9 teaches that we must be wary of even our own heartfelt estimation of what should or should not be expected of us in a given moment:

> The heart is deceitful above all things
>> and beyond cure.
> Who can understand it?

The key to discerning God's daily will for our lives is found in the following proverb:

> Trust in the LORD with all your heart
>> and lean not on your own understanding;
> in all your ways acknowledge him,
>> and he will make your paths straight. (Proverbs 3:5–6)

Jesus understood that God was the one who would provide balance for his life and make the wobbly path across the tightrope straight and sure. What a great promise and example for us! When we trust God in this way, we can let go of bitterness and blaming ("This rope is too flimsy!" "No one taught me how to do this!" "No one is helping me!") We stop rebelling against the situation, and relax into changing our attitude—the one thing we can control.

> But the fruit of the Spirit is love, joy, peace, patience, kindness, goodness, faithfulness, gentleness and self-control. Against such things there is no law. (Galatians 5:16–18, 22–23)

If after seeking to discern God's will, we realize we have been irresponsible in overcommitting, we can certainly make adjustments. We just need to check out our hearts before making any radical decisions to unload ourselves of responsibilities. Because Jeremiah is right in saying our hearts are deceptive, we will need to make such decisions by praying and by seeking advice from others.

Balance: The Right Yoke

Balance can also be defined as "stability produced by even distribution of weight on each side of the vertical axis." Think about a yoke ("a clamp or similar piece that embraces two parts to hold or unite them in position"). Jesus taught that we would find rest for our souls (balance!) if we would take his yoke upon us and learn from him (Matthew 11:28–30). Incredible: God is willing to clamp himself shoulder to shoulder with us, plowing through all life's burdens and dilemmas and pressures and disappointments—and joys—together. Wouldn't it be great to never get off track again because we simply could not stray away from God's path! However, like an unbroken horse in the wild, I can think sometimes that life is beautiful when I am free from any kind of yoke, even Jesus' yoke, which promises to be easy and light. Yet, true freedom only comes when we go God's way:

> I run in the path of your commands,
>   for you have set my heart free. (Psalm 119:32)

The Scriptures offer two possibilities for us: either we are yoked with Jesus or we are under a yoke of slavery to sin (Galatians 5:1). What gets us off balance? Getting ourselves strapped in under the wrong yoke. It's the nature of a yoke to be stronger than the animal that bears it—or else it would be of no use. It's hard to shake off the wrong yoke, but by following Jesus we can learn how to resist the wrong pressures and regain our equilibrium.

Selfish Ambition

The yoke of slavery to selfish ambition is a wrong yoke, and when working under this yoke, Christian women may struggle to give their families the time and attention they need. Strong, capable, ambitious women can have a hard time switching gears between job and children, ministry and family. The same is true for those of us who battle with insecurity: we enjoy the praise and recognition we get when we do a project well at work, when we study the Bible with someone who becomes a Christian, or when we as ministry leaders go off to visit another church somewhere; but often no one notices when we serve in the children's ministry or when we minister to our own children. Jesus warned people not to imitate the Pharisees, who loved recognition (Luke 20:46); he taught that we should not aspire to be the greatest, but rather the least among the brothers (Luke 9:46–48) and the greatest servant of all.

The entrance of children into our lives does seem to confuse us sometimes: Jesus' disciples rebuked people who brought children to him, absolutely misreading the Lord's intentions (Luke 18:15–16). Perhaps some of this confusion is due to our reluctance to be unworthy servants (Luke 17:10).

People-Pleasing

Jesus avoided the chafing yoke of slavery to people-pleasing. During the storm on the sea in Luke 8:22–24, Jesus slept while his friends were in mortal fear. His reply to their desperate cries for help was not, "Gee, sorry I wasn't here for you, guys!" but rather, "Where is your faith?" He was not focused on what they would think of him, which enabled him to speak the truth and call the disciples higher in their faith.

Desiring to Be in Control

Several of Jesus' friends were under the yoke of slavery to being in control: Martha was "worried and upset" and couldn't wait until Jesus' lesson was over to make preparations for the guests in her home (Luke 10:38–42). He spoke those gentle and convicting words, "Martha, Martha, you are worried and upset about many things, but only one thing is needed" (vv41–42), and thus brought balance back to her thinking.

When the people of a Samaritan village didn't welcome Jesus, his friends (James and John) were so upset they wanted to destroy them (Luke 9:54–55). Jesus rebuked the pair and moved on, unfazed, toward his goal of reaching Jerusalem. He had no desire to show his power simply to prove that he was in control of the situation.

Materialism and Comfort

We can get way out of balance under the yoke of slavery to materialism and comfort. Balance will not come from leading a comfortable life, surrounded by nice things. Jesus' story about the rich man and Lazarus teaches us that we shouldn't expect to receive only good things in this lifetime (Luke 16:25). Jesus declared that he would "suffer many things and be rejected by this generation" (Luke 17:25). We often run from pain and deny suffering, thinking that avoiding them will keep us in balance, but it turns out to be quite the opposite: God created us such that we must undergo suffering in order to mature and to grow toward perfection (Hebrews 5:8–9, James 1:2–3).

Balance: All or Nothing

> On one occasion an expert in the law stood up to test Jesus. Teacher," he asked, "what must I do to inherit eternal life?"
>
> "What is written in the Law?" he replied. "How do you read it?"
>
> He answered: "'Love the Lord your God with all your heart and with all your soul and with all your strength and with all your mind'; and, 'Love your neighbor as yourself.'"
>
> "You have answered correctly," Jesus replied. "Do this and you will live." (Luke 10:25–28)

Balance is also defined as "mental and emotional steadiness." And that steadiness comes only when we give our "all" to God, not our "some." As Jesus says above, "Do this and you will live." We might interpret, "Do this and you will be balanced."

Jesus was so steady that he managed to keep his heart engaged at all times.

> Soon afterward, Jesus went to a town called Nain, and his disciples and a large crowd went along with him. As he approached the town gate, a dead person was being carried out—the only son of his mother, and she was a widow. And a large crowd from the town was with her. When the Lord saw her, his heart went out to her and he said, "Don't cry." (Luke 7:11–13)

It's remarkable that Jesus had the emotional energy left, with all the demands upon him, to let his heart go out to this stranger. His love for God was so deep that he was able to pour himself out consistently on behalf of other people. When you love people very much, it rarely feels like a burden to do what you know will make them happy. It's easy to give it all when you're in love—and this was the way Jesus loved God.

Jesus fulfilled God's command: "whoever loves God must also love his brother" (1 John 4:21). It's clear that God expects us to be deeply involved in other people's lives. Consider this teaching: "If your brother sins, rebuke him, and if he repents, forgive him" (Luke 17:3). If you've ever been in a situation like this with a brother or sister, you know that this process will likely not take place in just a ten-minute conversation! "If he sins against you seven times in a day, and seven times comes back to you and says, 'I repent,' forgive him" (Luke 17:4). Now we're talking about the whole day being taken up with another person's sin and repentance. The disciples' response to this? "Increase our faith!" (Luke 17:5)

Jesus gave himself up completely to this "task" of loving God through loving the people around him. For him, there was no balance as we might seek it or imagine it for ourselves. But, in denying himself completely, loving God first and considering others better than himself (Philippians 2:3–9), he fulfilled the prophecy and promise of his own words, and "God exalted him to the highest place and gave him the name that is above every name." This paradox—that you have to keep pouring yourself out, not holding back, if you want balance—is the elusive truth that must become a conviction for women following Jesus. To paraphrase radio personality Dr. Laura Schlessinger, life is not a matter of balance, it's a matter of purpose. Everything in life has to be submitted to that purpose.

Our purpose is to draw close to God. Jesus gave us so many examples of how we might do this, practically—as in the story of the persistent widow in Luke 18. However, a lot of us following Jesus are not crying out to God day and night like that widow; we're too busy trying to bring balance into our lives by ourselves.

ৎ৯৵

If we want to live a truly balanced life, we must live in union with God and his will for our lives. If we are seeking balance first, rather than seeking the kingdom first, balance will always elude us. But if we trust him to work balance in our particular life situation—moment by moment and day by day—he will be faithful to that trust.

Group Session Three

Questions

1. After reading chapter 2, "Jesus Defines Balance," write a summary of what you learned from Jesus about how to find balance in life.

2. Do you sometimes find it difficult to relate to Jesus? Why or why not?

3. Did it frustrate you at all that by chapter 2 we are not yet into the "practicals" of getting balanced? Whether yes or no, why might we say that the truth stated in this chapter is the "horse" and the rest of the book is the "cart"?

4. Consider the following statement from page 35: "He was governed neither by [people's] desires nor his own desires. He was governed by God's desires for him at any given time and in any given place." How should this truth affect our seeking of balance? How has it been affecting you up until now? How do you need to change to become more like Jesus in this area?

Action Item

- Every day this week, no matter what is on your schedule or your to-do list, start your day by imitating Jesus and praying the following prayer:

  > "Father, in all I do today, help me to first seek to do your will—not to seek to please myself or to please others, but simply to please you."

Meeting Time

1. Share with each other your answers to each of the above questions.

2. Share what effect praying the above prayer in the morning had on you and your choices during the rest of the day.

3. Commit to read chapter 3, "God's Word: Our Balancing Pole," answer the questions, and do the action items before coming to the next meeting.

4. Pray together.

Remember Jesus' secret to maintaining his balance:
He often withdrew to lonely places and prayed.

chapter 3
God's Word: Our Balancing Pole

3

Kim Sapp
Atlanta, USA

Your word is a lamp to my feet
and a light for my path.

Psalm 119:105

*H*ave you ever watched a high-wire walker perform? What a breath-taking, heart-stopping spectacle it is—a feat of concentration, focus and balance. But did you know that the Old Testament has an account of a woman who was an excellent high-wire walker...a spiritual one, that is? We can imagine her in tights and sure-grip slippers as she walks confidently across the wire. The account is in Proverbs 31. We all know the woman: she cooks, she cleans, her career thrives, her family adores her and she never seems to break a sweat. Her perfection can make us want to pull our hair out! We want to be calm, peaceful, capable and never flustered; yet in reality, we are often harried, hurried, frazzled, frantic and just plain exhausted. Sometimes it's a struggle to just make it through a day, much less be righteous and spiritual in the process.

As women who are disciples of Jesus, we struggle to balance many different demands as we do our high-wire walk—relationship with God, family, evangelism, friends, career, housework—all while striving to live a righteous life. I realized early on that if I was going to survive as a Christian, I would have to find a spiritual center of balance. The world teaches women all the wrong solutions: Pamper yourself. Blame your husband. Buy something new. Get more sleep. And yet none of these "answers" strikes at the heart of the issue. The true solution lies in having a vibrant and consistent relationship with God.

After twenty-five years as a disciple of Jesus, I am convinced that Bible study and prayer are the keys to survival—not just in the spiritual battle, but also in life. When I first came to church as a college student, I was amazed by the Bible and what it had produced in the lives of the women around me. Once I became a Christian, I quickly began to rely on the Bible to balance my life—not only in handling my hectic schedule as a disciple, a student and a varsity athlete, but also in dealing with my own character and emotions.

These are some of the scriptures I clung to in those early days to keep me balanced:

> "But seek first his kingdom and his righteousness, and all these things will be given to you as well." (Matthew 6:33)

> Then he said to them all: "If anyone would come after me, he must deny himself and take up his cross daily and follow me. For whoever wants to save his life will lose it, but whoever loses his life for me will save it." (Luke 9:23–24)

> I can do everything through him who gives me strength. (Philippians 4:13)

Those scriptures were my inspiration, my hope and the foundation of my faith. At times they were the only solid things I could hold on to. As I have matured as a Christian and faced new stages of life, with their unique spiritual challenges, I have found different scriptures to help me through. When I look back over the last twenty-five years, the things I most remember—the markers of each significant time of my life—are the scriptures that helped me through each stage.

As a young wife and mother, living in the Bronx and raising two small children, I could not have survived without Psalm 86. As I taught my children to love God and become disciples of Jesus, I put my hope in 2 Timothy 1:5. When I endured challenges with my health, I depended on Job 33:14–30 and Job 42:12. For my marriage (and we have now been happily married for twenty years!) I look at 1 Peter 3:1–6 almost every day.

For more than twenty years, I dreamed the impossible—that somehow my dad, who was extremely set in his ways, could become a disciple. I read Luke 18:1–8 for twenty-three years and prayed for him daily until, in 1999, at the age of seventy-two, he was finally baptized into Christ! It is one of the greatest joys of my life to see him now, at seventy-five years old, as one of the most zealous members of our congregation.

Today I need God's word and prayer more than ever. I cannot remember the last time I didn't have a quiet time. I say this not out of arrogance, but out of desperation. I cannot survive a day without a time (or two) of prayer and a scripture to "balance" with. I now pray twice most days (notice the time of prayer at three in the afternoon in Acts 3:1). I also use two acronyms, HISGY and HISGT: How I Saw God Yesterday and How I Saw God Today. Both of these help me to look for God, to see how he has worked in my life and in others' lives, and to praise him.

Impossible Prayer List

I also pray daily through an "Impossible Prayer List," which is legendary in the Atlanta church. This list is comprised of five prayers that seem absolutely impossible—prayers that I present to God every day. God loves to hear and to answer these impossible prayers (Mark 10:27). In years past, my list has included my daughter and son and my mother-in-law and my father becoming disciples. Believe me, each of these prayers was impossible in my mind—and yet every one has now been answered! In Atlanta, countless disciples have seen family members become Christians, and nearly all of them were converted after these disciples spent much time pouring out their hearts to God with their Impossible Prayer Lists.

The written word of God is very powerful. In our house we practice Deuteronomy 6:9 literally: "write them on the doorframes of your houses and on your gates." Our kitchen has a four-foot-by-six-foot decorative chalkboard that usually has a scripture written on it. Everyone who visits is always interested to see what is written on the chalkboard. This week Psalm 91:14–16 has encouraged us as a friend of ours faced a serious operation. At different times I have written scriptures on the board in "honor" of each of my children. My favorite was the week of Proverbs 29:15: "The rod of correction imparts wisdom, but a child left to himself disgraces his mother." I had been allowing Jackson, my seven-year-old, to play outside with his friends too long without my attention, and this scripture reminded both of us of what was right.

Bible Study and Prayer

Another challenging aspect of balancing our lives is finding the balance between our Bible study and our prayer time. Most of us tend to focus too much on one element and neglect the other. Imagine a high-wire walker's balancing pole having one side heavier than the other—the walk would be even more difficult. Don't both ends of the pole need to be weighted evenly? So it should be with Bible study and prayer. Most women are usually drawn more to one or the other. I have always loved to pray; however, it is harder for me to study the Bible.

I have a theory about these tendencies: If you most love to pray and have a harder time reading the Bible, I suggest that you like to be open (prayer) but don't like to be discipled (Bible study). Conversely, if you love to read your Bible and prayer is more challenging for you, I suggest you like to be discipled (Bible study) and don't like to be open about your life (prayer). Test my theory to see if it holds true in your life. My friends and I have had a lot of fun with this theory, and it seems to be pretty accurate with most women. My friend Melinda says,

> I have to continually get back to having balanced times with God. What I mean is that sometimes I get on a reading spree, and I will read and read. Then I become out of touch, and I am not sure how I am doing because I haven't been praying and being open with God. Sometimes I swing the other direction and I pray a lot, but don't read. The result is an inconsistent faith, and I stop seeing God work in my life.

Focus Is the Key

Successful tightrope walkers have an extraordinary ability to focus. Certainly focus is an issue when trying to keep God and his word as the center of balance in our lives. I have chosen five "focus words" to help keep us balanced as we move through the different stages of our lives with God:

1. Discipline: Single Women
2. Desperation: Single Mothers
3. Decision: Wives and Mothers with Young Children
4. Determination: Wives and Mothers with Teenagers
5. Destiny: Wives and Mothers Whose Children Have Left Home

Discipline: Single Women

High-wire walkers must have intense discipline. Just to wear the form-fitting costumes, they are forever on a diet! Every step for them means success or failure. As a single woman, in many ways you are on your own. Your discipline in your relationship with God means life or death.

As young Christians, we had to develop the new habit of setting aside time for God every morning (following Jesus' example in Mark 1:35). When I was single, I was always busy doing great things for God, but I often forgot the greatest thing, which was to love God. Then I would wonder why I was struggling! A single friend of mine says,

> At times, I have gone days without quiet times. I have even turned my light on in my bedroom so my roommates would think I was having quiet times and would not ask me about it. The result from both (no relationship with God and a fake one) is the same: a powerless religion and a weak relationship with God.

Single women can be tempted to rely on themselves because they feel ultimate responsibility for their lives. And anytime we are relying upon ourselves, we are being prideful. We are thinking that somehow we can survive without God's help, and we become inconsistent in our times with God. Adding discipline to the zeal and energy of a single woman's relationship with God can make the difference between staying on the high wire and falling off.

Desperation: Single Mothers

I admire, respect and am amazed by all that single mothers do. Raising children is the hardest thing I have ever tried to do, and yet, I have help. The word "desperation" describes how single mothers whom I know feel most of the time. I remember our ministry in the Bronx and all the single mothers who became disciples. They had full-time jobs and multiple children; very few of them owned cars, and yet they were some of the most committed people in the church. Why? I believe it was because they were desperate and saw their need for God and the church. We have much to learn from these women who live such challenging lives but are so committed. A single mother in the Atlanta church writes,

> When I was asked to write about how I find time for Bible study and prayer, I was very humbled. This is a subject that has been a challenge for me. I rarely feel I spend enough time doing either. As a single working mom, there seems to be so little time for "quiet" anything. Typically, I spend a little time in the morning reading the word to set my thoughts, attitudes and especially my emotions. When I am struggling in an area, I write a scripture on an index card and read it throughout the day. Prayer comes in several forms. I have had to be humble when I have struggled in this area and have asked Christian friends to pray with me in the mornings. I also write out my prayers to help me focus. My favorite place to go is in the woods. Life seems to quiet down out there, and I can pour out my heart to my Father. I also pray throughout the day—short cries for help or things I have forgotten earlier.

I believe God gives a little extra help to single mothers. He helps them balance as they walk the high wire:

> He tends his flock like a shepherd:
>   He gathers the lambs in his arms
> and carries them close to his heart;
>   he gently leads those that have young. (Isaiah 40:11)

Decision: Wives and Mothers with Young Children

My husband, Steve, and I have often said that the biggest change in life comes when you have your first child. This is especially true for mothers. Your whole world is turned upside down and controlled by this precious baby. I remember shortly after my oldest child, Katherine, was born, I had to call a mature Christian friend to ask her how to have time with God—it didn't seem possible! She must have giggled to herself after she hung up...she has four children!

Making time with God after having a baby is a decision. No matter what time of day or night we manage to spend with God, we must decide to hang on to our relationship with him. The amount of time isn't even as important as the decision to remain consistent every day. A young mother in the Atlanta church describes the difficulties she has overcome:

> It is hard to find time to be with God, especially when your child is a newborn and you are exhausted all the time! You have to fight for time and use any little amount you can. The decision I made was to continue to make quiet times a priority in my life. I am a lot more creative and flexible with my relationship to God than I used to be. Now that my daughter is on a schedule, I can have a plan. I sometimes wake up thirty minutes before she does so I can pray. Then when she

is down for her morning nap, I can study my Bible. Then I might pray with a friend on the phone in the afternoon. I also do a lot more scripture memorization than I used to. I try to find one verse that speaks to me and repeat it to myself throughout the day. I find that I study the Gospels more because every sentence seems so full, and I can never study about Jesus too much. Even though I don't have as much time as I used to, I find that being a mother gives the scriptures even more meaning than they had before.

Another mother of young children says,

When you are a mother of young children, you have to make a daily decision to be self-controlled in order to have Bible time and prayer time. I have to put together a weekly plan. I think about what topics I will study, what DPI book I will read, and I update my prayer list. I find little corners of the house that I like to go to, places that allow me to concentrate and not daydream. The scripture "Be still and know that I am God" (Psalm 46:10) helps me to stop spinning, picking up toys and folding clothes. Instead of giving into the craziness of each day, I can make a decision to get a cup of tea, go to my corner and open my Bible and pray.

Determination: Wives and Mothers with Teenagers

And then teenagers enter the scene, throwing us completely off balance! "God, help all of us who are trying to raise them." When we see our sweet children grow up and develop their own sinful nature, we must be determined to depend on God to take us through these years victoriously. A mother of several teenagers says,

It's a fight to find time for Bible study and prayer. When my children were babies and toddlers, I wasn't coherent enough in the mornings to have my quiet times (sleep deprivation), but I had total control of my schedule. That allowed me to study and pray in the afternoons and during their nap times. However, it is not that easy, having two teens, one preteen and a part-time job that has me out the door by 8:30 five days a week. I've found that I have to be resolved to get up earlier in the mornings, which means getting to bed earlier the night before. There are car pools and errands and crazy schedules to accommodate. The bottom line for me is before I can do more *for* God, I need to do more *with* God.

Since entering the "mothers of teenagers" club, I have never had to pray more or be more determined to persevere and not give up. I have felt like I was falling off the high wire on a daily basis. One of the benefits of a great walk with God is that it cultivates the humility required to listen to and learn from other people. Counsel and encouragement from others have been crucial in helping me maintain my balance (and my sanity!) as my children have fought to develop their own relationships with God. Determination with God and your children will keep you walking on the high wire, and other people will help you to not fall off.

Destiny: Wives and Mothers Whose Children Have Left Home

What will *your* destiny be? Not your children's destiny, not your husband's destiny, but yours? Now that your children are gone, you have more time to think about it. But be careful! Reaching a more mature stage of life should not mean spiritual rest or retirement. Just because our children leave us does not mean that Satan will leave us alone. As we get older, Satan invents new tactics to distract and harm us. He still tries to make us fall off the high wire—even when we are closer to the other side. Listen to the heart of friend of mine:

As an "empty nester" who has recently retired, I now have more uninterrupted time in the mornings for studying the Word and praying. I thought when I reached this point, I would no longer need to be as disciplined as when I had children at home and worked, but that has not been the case. As we age, Satan works on us in different ways. We are warned in 2 Peter 1:5–9 that we must increase in our self-control as we grow older. God knows that unless we make "every effort" in this area, we will succumb to the natural laziness, apathy, worry and self-absorption common to our age.

No matter what our age or situation in life, staying on the high wire is a fight. God will help us to keep our balance until the very end if we make the effort to stay close to him.

We cannot know our specific destiny or predict our future, but one thing is sure: God's plan for each of us is to grow ever closer to him throughout our lives. Our relationship with him is by far his greatest gift and is the key to living a meaningful, fulfilling and balanced life. Through discipline, desperation, decision, determination and a sense of destiny, our walk with God can help us not only to survive the high-wire walk of life, but to also be victorious. And we do not have to walk fearfully, dreading every step (although we will all have our scary moments!). Closeness to God helps us walk with confidence and courage, knowing our walk is an adventure—and we can love every minute of it!

Group Session Four

Questions

1. After reading chapter 3, "God's Word: Our Balancing Pole," think back through your life and the key scriptures that have sustained you spiritually.

2. Which aspect of your relationship with God do you find easier, Bible study or prayer? Read again Kim's theory on this subject (page 51). How accurate is the theory in your life?

3. Look back over the five "D" words that Kim lists. Which one most relates to your life—even if it is listed with someone in a different life situation than yours? Why?

Action Items

- Commit to a specific theme of Bible study for the time between now and your next Balance Group meeting. Be consistent every day in following through with this study.

- Through prayer, come up with an Impossible Prayer List, and begin to pray daily about these requests.

Meeting Time

1. Share with each other your answers to each of the above questions.

2. Share your theme of Bible study coming into the group, and let the group know how consistent you were throughout the week.

3. Share with the group your Impossible Prayer List.

4. Commit to read chapter 4, "Live Out Your Priorities," answer the questions, and do the action items before coming to the next meeting.

5. Pray together.

Remember that closeness to God helps us walk with confidence and courage. Enjoy the adventure.

chapter 4
Live Out Your Priorities

4

Terrie Fontenot
Washington, USA

> "Martha, Martha," the Lord answered, "you are worried and upset about many things, but only one thing is needed. Mary has chosen what is better, and it will not be taken away from her."
>
> Luke 10:41–42

First things first." I can still hear those words ringing in my ears. How many times did my parents say them? I don't know, but it was a lot! These words, along with many others, were an attempt to train me in setting priorities in my life. There were some fundamental principles that they were trying to instill in me, such as, "Work now and play later." I am thankful for this repetitious direction that has helped me to "get the job done" so many times in my life.

As a disciple of Jesus, I must constantly evaluate the importance of the work I am doing as I imitate the Lord. It is easy for me to be busy, but not really working at what God would consider the first priority. Our first-century sister Martha found herself in the same predicament in Luke 10:38–42. She definitely understood *working* before *playing*. And she surely thought that Mary was *playing* when she should have been *working*—but she was wrong. Jesus clarifies it when he says, "Mary has chosen what is better, and it will not be taken away from her." Martha had gotten her priorities back to front. How often does this happen to us? Unfortunately, it is easy to do.

I'm a keep-it-simple kind of a gal. When things are too complex, I get overwhelmed. I just don't have the brainpower to figure out all the details and keep everything straight. Thankfully, our God understands such limitations, and he likes to keep it simple as well. He sets the priorities for our lives as his children, and he gives us the power and the resources to live them out.

In Matthew 22:34–40, Jesus prioritizes God's commands. A Pharisee asked Jesus this question: "Teacher, which is the greatest commandment in the Law?" And Jesus replied:

> "'Love the Lord your God with all your heart and with all your soul and with all your mind.' This is the first and greatest commandment. And the second is like it: 'Love your neighbor as yourself.' All the Law and the Prophets hang on these two commandments."

Here Jesus basically boils the whole Bible down to its essential elements. Focus on two things: *loving God* and *loving people*. The rest is all an elaboration on how to do these two things effectively. This scripture sets our priorities for us and keeps them clear and firm. All our time, activities, motivations and goals need to be encompassed in these two commands. Our lives are to be anchored on these two commands. When life gets complicated and overwhelming, we must go back to these foundational teachings that hold everything in its place. When we are accepting the world's view of priorities for our life—usually putting self and personal achievement at the top—our foundation becomes weak, our rope goes slack and we lose our balance quickly.

Alpha and Omega

Our relationship with God has to be the first priority in our lives in order to achieve balance of any kind. It is an all-encompassing relationship, as we can see from the first commandment above. Our schedules must reflect the importance of this relationship, as was explained so well in the previous chapter.

In Luke 10:27 Jesus refers to these same two commandments when a lawyer asks him how to have eternal life. Jesus tells the man, "Do this and you will live." The lawyer required more explanation about who his neighbor was, and thus follows the Parable of the Good Samaritan. I think it is interesting to note that immediately following this lesson, Jesus had his now-famous visit with Mary and her sister, Martha. Mary chose what was "better," yet the guests were still hungry. Certainly Jesus would not have had Mary ignore her visitors and not see to their needs. His teaching that day spoke more to getting our basic priority straight before we attempt to do the right things for people. So, after we emerge from our time with God, it is time to then pour that love into the people surrounding us.

As disciples, we have numerous relationships, and we must prioritize them. We are all different and have different talents, personalities, intellect, backgrounds, roles and the list goes on. But there is one thing in which we are all equal: we all have twenty-four hours in a day. Rich people cannot buy more; artistic people cannot create more; persuasive people cannot coax more. How we choose to use our time makes all the difference in the quality of our lives. While we live out our priorities, we make choices that affect us and affect those close to us. As I continue to minister to women, a phrase I hear often is, "I don't have time." Then following this phrase are all the things that they think they should do or would like to do. Too often we are caught up in what Charles Hummel calls the "tyranny of the urgent."[1] We have lost control of our schedules and they have begun to control us. We often feel trapped and at a loss about how to get free.

We need to take responsibility for what we do with our time. We need to make choices, be content with them and then trust God. Does this sound like a tall order to you? It is a lifelong pursuit—lived out a day at a time. We are creatures of habit. The great thing about being human, however, is that we can train ourselves to establish godly habits. The simple exercise of keeping a priority planner each week helps me to ingrain in my mind lifelong, habitual ways of thinking and planning. These priorities are simple. For single women: God, family, friends (disciples and nondisciples). For married women: God, husband, children, friends (disciples and nondisciples). I plan each week for the needs in all these relationships.[2]

The One My Heart Loves

For married women, our number one priority, after God, is our husband. It sounds simple, but as I interviewed various women in preparation for writing this chapter, I found it to be more difficult than we may think. It is challenging not to give in to our selfish and sinful natures, even when it comes to the person who means the most to us. A friend I spoke to who is married without children, said she finds herself giving her husband the "leftovers" in her energy and emotions, after the people at work and in her ministry.

Another friend, who has several older children, has been married for many years and has an exemplary marriage, expressed this: "My

---

[1] Charles Hummel, *Tyranny of the Urgent* (Downers Grove, Ill.: InterVarsity Press, 1994).
[2] I did not list "job" as a priority (though it is) because I am primarily dealing with priorities in relationships. Certainly the relationships at your job are included in this consideration of relational priorities.

husband needs me and I need him. Sometimes I don't want this to be a priority, but this is right and always good." We all have to fight the desire to be selfish and to consider our own needs first, forgetting that the command is to love others *as* we love ourselves.

I have seen women mess up the balance in their marriage by not keeping their husband as their number one relationship. Yet, as we know, wives can become disappointed, hurt, disillusioned and even bitter in their relationship with their husbands. This is how it typically happens: Our greatest need in the marriage relationship is love, just as the greatest need for the man is respect (Ephesians 5:33). When our need for love is not met by our husband, it is easy to begin to look elsewhere. We may turn to a close friend or two, or if a woman has children, she may begin to pour all her emotion and devotion into them in order to feel loved and appreciated. And let's just say that when Mom is trying to have her emotional needs met by the children, life is out of balance! Children become spoiled and a source of conflict in the marriage. Mom tries to protect them from Dad, whom she sees as unloving. Unity is destroyed. The children become insecure because the foundation is shaking. Priorities need to be reestablished and God's order reintroduced into the family.

We can keep our marriage balanced by not neglecting the physical, sexual, emotional and spiritual needs of our husband. Plan each week to do something to strengthen your marriage. Think daily how you can encourage your man. Be sure to ask him what will encourage him because we can think we know—and be completely wrong! We should never assume he needs the same things we need. We must make time to talk to each other every day, which can often be neglected in our busy lives. This may seem obvious, but I have found that most couples do not sit down and just talk on a regular basis. We need conversation time with just the two of us, eyeball-to-eyeball, uninterrupted. Most couples I know do not do this for even fifteen or twenty minutes a day. Unfortunately, their marriage reflects this kind of neglect. The relationship is not being nurtured and therefore is not growing. We need to put this time into our priority planners.[3]

A woman I admire greatly in our church is married, has two small children, works a full-time job outside the home and spiritually oversees the women in a region of a hundred people. Angela is very calm, peaceful and gentle. She has a great sense of strength and balance in her life. I would like to quote some of her thoughts here on a balanced life and setting priorities.

> When I think of balance, I think of walking on a balance beam, or standing on one leg—you need a focal point to do that, something to concentrate on. In the spiritual sense, my focal point needs to be God, and then everything else will balance out: my time spent with God, my husband, my children, my job, my ministry and my time keeping my house in order. All this will be held together as long as I am looking into the face of God. What a balanced life *doesn't* look like is chaotic, unorganized, stressful, etc. A balanced life should result in peace. Not that there aren't things thrown in our way to cause us to struggle and to lose our focus—but once focus is regained, the stress subsides, the chaos drifts away and there is peace—because God is in control.
>
> Since I work during the day, I definitely have to have a good schedule to follow so that I have enough time with my children, as well as being involved in the ministry, as well as keeping the house in a way that is welcoming for hospitality. I schedule my Bible studies with friends after the kids go to sleep (typically) so that I can spend

---

[3] You may not be able to get your husband to actually sit down to talk to you. Many men like to be active while conversing, so you may need to plan to do something else while talking. My husband and I often take a walk and talk. I find it helps us to get out of the house. The point is, do anything you can to make it happen and make it a habit (without being a nag!).

time with them before they go to bed. We try to have the Bible studies at our house if we can. If both my husband and I have studies on the same night, we try to have one parent at home doing a study, while the other is out. A lot of communication needs to be involved in setting up your schedules when you are married, or else there will be a lot of conflicts. (I have learned from experience.)

When I start to feel like I am never at home, I definitely struggle with that. Making sure my family is taken care of is definitely high on the list, because ultimately, my children are my first ministry, and my goal is for them to make it to heaven.

Impress upon Your Children

As married women, after our relationship with God and then our husband, the relationships we should consider our next priority would be our children. For single moms, our next priority after our relationship with God should be our children. The command Jesus gave in Matthew 22 to love God wholeheartedly was first given in Deuteronomy 6:4–8, where it is immediately followed by the admonition to "impress them on your children." In Deuteronomy 6:2, it states that the commands were given

> ...so that you, your children and their children after them may fear the LORD your God as long as you live by keeping all his decrees and commands that I give you, and so that you may enjoy long life.

Loving God and our neighbor are the utmost priorities, and then God shows us how to pass these priorities on to future generations:

> Talk about them when you sit at home and when you walk along the road, when you lie down and when you get up.

> Tie them as symbols on your hands and bind them on your foreheads. Write them on the doorframes of your houses and on your gates. (Deuteronomy 6:7–9)

When we live like this, there is the promise of "long life." Additionally, Proverbs 22:6 gives us further admonition in this area, saying, "Train a child in the way he should go, and when he is old he will not turn from it." God expects us to be training our children in how to love him completely. It is more than just outward obedience to commands—the command is to *love*. We, as parents, must train the hearts of our children, not just their behavior. And God is very specific about how this is to be done: consistently, throughout the day, in whatever we are doing.

In other words we are to bring God's commandments right into our daily lives. We are to use life situations to teach and train our children in the fear and wonder of God. I have known parents to only bring out the Scriptures for punishment or rebuking, but this is not what God is saying here. We need to understand how God thinks about every aspect of our lives and consider his ways. These are to be impressed on our children "24/7." We are also to write scriptures down and have them close at hand to meditate on and memorize. This is something to consider as we train our children: are we really teaching them the Scriptures?

The promise in Proverbs 22 is a conditional one. We must do our part in the training of our children. Training, for anything, takes a lot of time and focus if we want to be successful. Our children, who God has entrusted to us, deserve this time and focus. We should be very clear on our objectives and goals in the training of our children. If we are lacking direction, no training is going on, or I should say, no *spiritual* training is going on—the world is always directing our children! We only have our children with us for a short time, and there is much to teach them. We cannot afford to be slack, letting time pass and allowing the world to make a greater impression on them than the word of God. They need a strong foundation in their lives if they are going to keep their balance on life's tightrope.

Prayer and Perseverance

I believe to train our children well, we must be women of prayer. We need to pray a lot *for* our children and *with* our children. Pray to have the eyes of God, to focus on the greatest needs of your children. Pray to see how you can impress his commands on their hearts. Pray for perseverance, patience and lots of unconditional love. God will always answer these prayers.

The other admonition from this passage in Deuteronomy is to "never give up." We must continue to be women of faith, not giving in to fear and discouragement. Raising children is a long battle, and we cannot become weary in doing good. Use the "village" God has given you to raise your children. From week to week, in your priority planner, be sure to think and plan for the needs of your children. Have goals and objectives to achieve, appropriate to their stage of development. Learn how to apply Deuteronomy 6 on a daily basis. Break it down. Have family devotionals each week, and make them fun. Teach your children to pray in thankfulness and to pray through all fears.

Let me share with you the thoughts of a balanced woman and great friend of mine, Jean.

As a mother of a teen, my priority is to encourage my teen to have good relationships with disciples, to be in the Word regularly, to spend time with those who can help him grow spiritually, and to initiate in different areas of his life. Much of my encouragement is in the form of personal example in these areas. I make an effort to have functions in my home with teens and their parents. I need relationships with the other parents of teens too. I try to help my teen to be spiritually fruitful by reaching out to the parents of his friends. I also want to help develop his talents, so I try to give him opportunities to experience and try new areas of interest. I want my children to keep a good relationship with grandparents, so I encourage visits, cards and phone calls. I stay on top of their grades and talk to counselors and teachers when needed. And I have been training my children to do their part, such as cleaning their rooms and bathrooms, plus general house cleaning as needed. They did their own laundry once they were in middle school. This helps them in learning responsibility.

Jean is definitely a woman who focuses, plans and considers all aspects of her family's needs. At this writing, all three of her children are strong disciples of Jesus.

Dinnertime

Family dinnertime was always a very important and special occasion in our home. I had dinner prepared most evenings at the same time. Everyone knew the time and could plan other activities accordingly. Table fellowship is historically an important aspect of strong family life in the Bible, and we have seen the wisdom of this through the years. It was a time for us to always connect with each other after a busy day. The conversation was always lively. Sometimes we played games or had Bible trivia. The children would tell us their latest jokes and interesting experiences. It was also a time of training. We helped our children with their social skills. They learned etiquette and manners. We used this time to help them sort out their relationship issues. We all have fond memories of meal times together.

My friend Jean is married to a physician and has to keep an organized but flexible schedule. Let's learn from what she has to say:

Setting my priorities starts early in the week and includes communicating with my family. I try to write things down on the calendar. Here are some of the convictions and good habits I have learned:

- Spending good time with Christians weekly, in my home and in theirs

- Speaking to my neighbors weekly

- Calling my parents and children weekly

- Not leaving the house until the bed is made and hopefully the dishes are done

- Not leaving the house until I have had time with God

- Initiating sexually with my husband at least weekly

- Having consistent family times on Mondays (We have protected these over the years.)

- Consolidating meetings on the same days as much as possible, leaving free times for reach-out times and family times

- Trying to grab a few minutes daily, either before dinner or after, to talk privately with my husband

- Sharing good news or scriptures with each other throughout the week—at the dinner table is a good time

Things to say "no" to:

- Allowing sports or activities to become all-consuming (I do want my children to be involved in things, but not to the point that it becomes their main focus and everything else must be worked around it. I hope they will take this mentality into adulthood.)

- Anything interfering with family times (We trained the children in this at a very early age; they don't even ask to compromise.)

- Things we can change if my husband and I need to get close

- Phone calls during quiet times and dinnertimes

There are numerous books written on training our children, but hopefully this has been enough to stimulate your thinking and creativity in training your children. Create the memories that will be impressed on them forever. Not all memories will be good, but they can all be useful for training. Someone once said, "Growing old is inevitable, but growing up is optional," but this is not true for children we hope to influence with the gospel![4]

Singles and Family

One of the greatest dangers for single women is to become self-centered. You really only have yourself to consider about many practical things in life, which can be positive or negative. Of course, as Christian single women, you know that denying yourselves is the way to live. One area to evaluate to see if you are being balanced like Jesus is in your relationships with your physical family members—your parents,

---

[4] A great book on parenting is published by DPI: *Raising Awesome Kids* by Sam and Geri Laing (Billerica, Mass.: Discipleship Publications International, 1994).

siblings or extended family. Moms and dads generally still want to be a part of their children's lives, no matter how old they are. Brothers and sisters can feel neglected and unimportant if we do not make efforts to stay in touch. It is important to remember birthdays, special occasions and just those phone calls that say, "I was thinking of you." For example, you can share memories you have as a family or news in your lives—anything that keeps you connected. We have many friends, but only one physical family. These are unique relationships that only you have. Your mom and dad may have many friends, but only their children can be their children. Take the time to be in touch regularly and stay as close as possible to the family God gave you.

The Family of God

As we organize our time, whether we are singles or marrieds or parents, we think next of other disciples of Jesus. We must set aside times to spend with others who encourage and strengthen us, and also for those who need our encouragement and strength. Both kinds of relationships are essential in order for us to have a healthy, balanced life. I read an article recently about a study done on stress and women. The two greatest forms of stress release for women are caring for children and talking with a good friend. As I reflected on that, I found it to be quite true in my own life. There is nothing like taking care of children to get my mind off things or talking with a close friend to dispel all those fears and burdens I have been carrying, especially if I can have a good cry as well. Therefore, it's not just about making time to give to others, but making time to share ourselves with others, too.

Jean and I recently took a road trip. We traveled for five days and went to see my two daughters in one college and then traveled to another state to see her college-age daughter. We then traveled to another state to see my married daughter, and Jean caught up with some of her old friends. We then drove back to Virginia, stayed the night at her parents' home and headed back the next day. We never turned on the radio—we literally talked for days. When I arrived home, I wasn't really tired; I felt quite relaxed. We all need spiritual women in our lives to talk to. Put it in your planner.

When We Get Off Track

I asked a single friend of mine to describe her life when it is going "off track." Cindy is a lawyer with a very demanding job. She travels a great deal and also leads a single women's ministry. She is one of the most organized women I know. This is how she describes her life when it is unbalanced:

- Personal appearance becomes unkempt (don't have energy to do hair, make-up, etc.)

- Car and house are messy; laundry builds up

- Feelings of resentment and feeling the need to blame someone; feeling self-piteous

- Easily frustrated; crying easily

- Little personal and social life

- Feeling negative and hopeless, not wanting to think about my future

- Few groceries in the house; skipping meals—craving sugar

- Bills going unpaid

- Lots of phone calls and e-mails unreturned

It is good to identify the signs when we are falling off the tightrope. It is also good to have friends who are "spotting" for us and can let us know when we are wobbling. It is wise to ask for this help regularly, as we are often blind to our shortcomings.

Time As Blocks

The following is a list of how my friend Cindy plans her time. She keeps balanced by looking at time in blocks—month by month and week by week. On Sunday or Monday she plans what she'd like to accomplish by considering the following:

1. Find out when non-Christians can study the Bible.

2. Find out availability of weak disciples and/or emergency discipling situations.

3. Schedule set deadlines and meetings.

4. Plan work.

5. Plan remaining ministry responsibilities; set up times with Christian friends for challenge and encouragement.

6. Plan social time.

7. Schedule personal time.

Planning makes all the difference for reaching the goals we set out to accomplish. We all know that being prepared makes the journey smooth. You just can't walk a tightrope without the necessary equipment and everyone in their place. Make sure the people in your life have a place in keeping you up there.

'Inviting in' Strangers

Throughout our lives, of course, we have a mission: to help others to know God. If I am not studying the Bible with someone, I feel aimless and a little out of touch. I think it is good that I feel that way, because at that point I am beginning to become that way—aimless and out of touch. I have many roles to play and many things I do in this life, but I have only one mission. No matter what is going on in my life, my mission is to help others to know God. I believe that throughout our lives, God gives us opportunities to fulfill this mission. As long as we keep our eyes and mouths open, we will be able to speak and teach about him. As we spend time with our family and friends, we can easily share with others the treasure that God has given us. It only brings us closer to our family and friends and helps us set an example in training our children by living out the priorities God has set for us. So when we are planning, we must be sure to include the people God has put in our path to talk to.

We have always had non-Christians over for dinner and shared our family with them. Those times have been more helpful than almost anything else in building the faith of our friends. All our life with God is to be shared. Our children have learned to reach out and give to people in this way. I believe their prayers have been more effective in saving some of these lost souls than mine. Don't rob yourself of this great joy God has provided for your life.

A woman I appreciate for her heart for strangers is Kim. She is married and a mother of three. She makes the most of all opportunities. She has recently studied the Bible with three wonderful women: a neighbor who has cancer, the woman who coordinates all the soccer events in Virginia Beach and the mother of a young, single woman she just baptized. Kim is a "soccer mom"; in fact, she is a soccer coach for her youngest son's team. Her oldest son recently became a Christian. One of the very inspiring things about his baptism was seeing the impact he has had on people of all ages. His soccer coach came to his baptism, is now coming to church, and the coach and his wife are interested in studying the Bible with Kim and her husband. Kim is a great mom who is always about her mission, and her children are learning to do the same.

Remember, *first things first*. Love God and love people. Even in her frustration, Martha knew to turn to the Lord for help. Keep it simple, stay limber and flexible and don't ever jump off the tightrope! "All things are possible with God" (Mark 10:27): we *can* live out our priorities and all be great spiritual funambulists.

Group Session Five

Questions

1. After reading chapter 4, "Live Out Your Priorities," write out the specific roles that you play in the lives of other people. (i.e., wife, mom, supervisor, employee, family-group leader, etc.) Pray about being committed in all these areas, and decide to trust that God will help you be faithful.

2. If you are married, write out a response to Terrie's sections about loving your husband and your children. Which point is the most needed in your life right now? Why?

3. If you are single, write out a response to Terrie's section about loving your family. What commitment do you need to make to be faithful to your family? What is your greatest challenge in this area? How can God help you overcome this challenge?

4. We all need friends in our lives—both disciples and nondisciples. How do you want to grow and change in being more faithful to your friends who are Christians? To your friends who are not Christians?

Action Items

• In planning your next week, write out one goal for each area of relational responsibility. (See the chart on the following page.)

• Follow through with your goals and be ready to share with the group how it went.

Relationship	Goal
Wife	Leave encouraging voice-mail message at work for my husband
Mom	Take children to park on Wednesday
Daughter	Call Mom on Tuesday
Sister	Send clipping from home newspaper
Supervisor	Birthday card for Sarah
Friend	Ask Leslie how her new job is going
Family-group leader	Send out special scripture by e-mail to group
Etc.	

Meeting Time

1. Share with each other your answers to each of the above questions and discuss.

2. Share how you did with your relational goals for the week.

3. Discuss what signs in your life show you that your priorities are out of balance.

4. Commit to read chapter 5, "Keep Your Eyes on Jesus," answer the questions, and do the action item before coming to the next meeting.

5. Pray together.

Remember that your schedule should
reflect what you say your priorities are.

chapter 5
Keep Your Eyes on Jesus

5

Barbara Porter
Saõ Paulo, Brazil

*T*here I was with my planner opened before me, attempting to neatly fit in the different plans and activities I wished to accomplish that week. Then an unexpected, unassuming little e-mail found its way into my computer. It was the invitation to write a chapter in this book about having a balanced life. It came the day after I had agreed to direct an Easter play that would have performances almost every weekend in the month of March.

The e-mail explained that my chapter, if I accepted, would be due on March 26. I perused the various options of chapter themes, and my eyes were quickly drawn to the one that dealt with "How to say no without feeling guilty." Bingo! I could say no to writing the chapter without feeling guilty! Isn't that the whole point of the balanced life? Priorities? Not biting off more than you can chew? Doing what you do excellently instead of doing everything halfway? I confess I felt quite justified in my desire to refuse this invitation. Besides, was I really the best one for the job? Was I not constantly questioning my own ability to keep all the plates spinning as a wife, mother, Christian, church leader, daughter, friend, etc.? And who, besides Martha Stewart, really thinks they have a balanced life anyway? However, wanting to make sure I was following

God's direction (one of the points we will soon discuss), I sought some advice and decided to accept the assignment.

Let us start with the tightrope analogy, the theme illustration of this book. Our friend is holding her pole, trying not to fall into the chasm below. Where does she look? Does she gaze at her boyfriend who is blowing her a kiss? Does she wave to her mom who gloats proudly on the sidelines? Does she smile at the photographer who begs to take her picture? Not if she wants to stay on the rope! She keeps her eyes fixed on her focal point. She understands that if she takes her eyes off of that point, she will fall—and it will not be pretty.

Aren't we relieved that life is not really a tightrope that spans a great chasm? It sure feels like it sometimes, though, doesn't it? Some of us feel like any slightly wrong move will cause us to plummet to disaster, as though it were the end of the world. We cling so tightly to what we believe to be God's agenda for us that God has to pry our schedules out of our hands to get some control over them. In contrast, others of us are so quick to get distracted, to drop our poles, to look everywhere but the focal point—anything and everything *but* Jesus clamors for our attention.

Hebrews 12:1–3 gives us some great insight. Think about how to apply these verses to your life as you are reading:

> Therefore, since we are surrounded by such a great cloud of witnesses, let us throw off everything that hinders and the sin that so easily entangles, and let us run with perseverance the race marked out for us. Let us fix our eyes on Jesus, the author and perfecter of our faith, who for the joy set before him endured the cross, scorning its shame, and sat down at the right hand of the throne of God. Consider

him who endured such opposition from sinful men, so that you will not grow weary and lose heart.

Fix Our Eyes on Jesus

How does our friend make it across the chasm? She fixes her eyes on a fixed point—no matter what! In the same way, we must keep our eyes fixed on Jesus and his example if we want to stay balanced in our lives. What does this mean?

In Hebrews 12:1–3, the writer tells us that Jesus had a clearly defined goal: endure the cross so that he would be able to joyfully sit down "at the right hand of the throne of God." He would allow absolutely nothing to keep him from this goal. For example, Jesus would not allow a worldly sense of justice—"This isn't fair!"— to rescue him from the cross. Therefore, he refused to defend himself before the high priest and before Pilate, knowing that he had done no wrong and that the charges against him were groundless. Jesus also knew that his enemies considered his dying on a cross a great defeat for the so-called Savior. Yet, he was convinced that the cross would lead to his most victorious moment, the resurrection. Then he rebuffed Satan's last earthly temptation: to fold under the pressure of the mocking and scorn he endured while hanging on the cross. Jesus refused to give in! His focal point in life, what drove him to dominate every temptation he faced, was to painfully die on that cross, be separated from his Father and rise in triumph on the third day.

For me, fixing my eyes on Jesus means deciding to do what is right, no matter how hard or painful it is. Thankfully, most of us will never experience the physical pain of dying on a cross. But to truly follow in the footsteps of Jesus, loving unconditionally as he did, is no easy task. In fact, many times, the right thing is also the hardest. I remember when a weak Christian contemptuously accused me of something I had not done, and everything in me wanted to defend myself and challenge her on her bad attitudes. However, it was obvious that she was very upset, so I apologized that certain decisions that had been made had hurt and confused her. At that point, the only thing that motivated me to do what was right was the example of Jesus on the cross and how he submitted to such unjust treatment on behalf of me, a sinner. Fixing my eyes on Jesus helped me not do what I *felt* like doing, but to do what would be best for the person at that moment.

If, like Jesus, our primary purpose in life is "to run with perseverance the race marked out for us" (Hebrews 12:1) and get ourselves and as many as possible to heaven, we can fix our eyes on Jesus by being determined not to compromise our priorities. A friend of mine, Leslie, came to Saõ Paulo with the mission team. She married one of the first Brazilian converts and presently lives in Saõ Paulo, where she works full-time and has two preteen children. Leslie offers some very practical advice about maintaining her priorities:

> I leave my Bible out, opened up to where I've already decided that I'll read, the night before. How can I choose a load of laundry over that? Matthew 6:33 is probably the most valuable insight in this entire balance quest. "Seek first the kingdom of God and his righteousness..." and all the rest will eventually fall into place. And even if it doesn't, who cares? You're going to heaven!

Celia, a mother of four (a preteen and three teens) who works part-time in her husband's business adds,

It helps me to know that, like Jesus, I have no choice. I can't go backwards because I won't be able to see the tightrope. I can't just stop because sooner or later, I will surely fall. One thing I am sure of—I want to be with God and please God. So since I don't want to fall, I have to go forward. I am confident and secure, trusting that God will help me walk toward him, even in the midst of problems and challenges.

It strengthens Celia to remember she is not alone. Neither are we! As we continue along our Christian journey, let us not forget that God is always there and provides us with "everything we need for life and godliness" (2 Peter 1:3).

Focus on the Joy Set Before Us

Hebrews 12 refers to the "joy set before us." Sometimes, although the joy is set "before" us, we don't want to wait for it. Like a spoiled child, we stomp our feet and say to God, "Daddy, I want it *now*!" Jesus set his sights on the joy he would experience *after* he died on the cross. That joy was part of Jesus' motivation. Had Jesus been walking the tightrope, he would have been focused on his Father's welcoming embrace at the end of the rope and then the joy of having completed his mission.

Let's face it, this requires tremendous patience of which our supply is often short. When was the last time you saw a tightrope walker running—or even walking fast? If we live for immediate gratification, even in the spiritual sense, we may miss the mark of the balanced life. Let us consider that indeed part of the joy set before us is the patience God will add to our character.

We must also have deep convictions about what truly brings us joy. If it is the desire of our hearts to please God, we will derive joy from the mere fact that God is more pleased with a godly heart than he is with our performance. Suedine, mother of a one-year-old, says that in seeking a joyful attitude, she tries not to be overwhelmed by her responsibilities, but rather, focuses on being grateful for the privilege of having to do all that she does (which includes working full-time and caring for her family, as well as serving in many ways in the church). Patricia, mother of three children, all disciples, specifically asks God for the joy to do the things she least enjoys doing.

We must believe that God is more pleased when we trust him than when we get everything just right. This is truly great news! Remember Mary and Martha? In Luke 10:38–42, Martha hurriedly (dare I say frantically?) worked to get the cooking and cleaning done. She was growing weary and losing heart because things were not happening the way she wanted them to. Mary sat listening at Jesus' feet. Then, to add insult to injury, when Martha complained about Mary not helping her, fully expecting Jesus to come to her defense, Jesus replied, "Martha, Martha, you are worried and upset about many things, but only one thing is needed. Mary has chosen what is better, and it will not be taken away from her" (Luke 10:41–42).

I am often guilty of being a Martha. And what is worse, like Martha, I expect Jesus to defend me! I justify my anxiety by calling it "intensity." I am ashamed to confess, I sometimes get impatient with others who are not trying to get as much done as I am. My very wonderful and patient husband not only stops to correct this very prideful attitude, but also encourages me to stop and smell the roses. He helps me to see that if my goal is truly to glorify God, I will be more focused on having a joyful heart than a perfect "finished product," even if this means sandwiches instead of filet mignon. What our Lord describes as "better," the only thing that is needed, "that which will not be taken away" is intimacy with him. Good things like our God-given daily responsibilities and even our desire for excellence should never be allowed to hinder our joyful and intimate relationship with Jesus.

Foster Flexibility

How do you feel about interruptions? You have your day or week all planned out. You have allowed just enough time (perhaps a little extra) to get everything done. Then comes the call, the sickness, the visit, the need, and you wonder, "Now what? How will I get this all done?"

The Israelites traveling toward the Promised Land essentially had their planners filled out by God himself. The Bible describes the complete clarity of God's guidance of the Israelites: by day, God led his people in a cloud; by night, God appeared to his people in a pillar of fire. As we read in Numbers 9:15–23, God had trained his people to pack up and move whenever he decided it was time. They then settled camp whenever God settled over the tabernacle. I am amazed by the flexibility of God's people. The Bible teaches that sometimes the people stayed encamped for months, but sometimes they stayed for just a few days.

Most of us as women like to plan. We like to have all our ducks in a row. We want to know exactly what will happen, at what time, where and with whom. But God trained the Israelites to be totally dependent on his guidance and flexible to his leading. I can just imagine myself in the middle of making dinner and hearing that the cloud has lifted.

"It's time to go!" I hear the Levite priests cry out. Would I calmly stop what I was doing to express overflowing gratitude that God was making his will for my life clear? I doubt it! More likely, I would be thinking, "Couldn't he give us a little warning? I just finished hanging the pictures in the tent! Does he expect me to just stop what I'm doing to move out? It's just not fair...." And whatever iota of joy I had left would go out through the tent flap.

What the passage in Numbers teaches us is to look at interruptions as divine—allowed by our sovereign God and not part of a conspiracy to frustrate our lives. God permits interruptions and even disruptions to teach us to trust in his perfect plan for our lives. God wants us to depend on *him,* not on what we may think is best. More importantly, he wants us to trust him joyfully, not just bite our tongue and endure, but truly experience the peace that comes from completely submitting our will to his.[1]

Betina, single mother of an eleven year old, has been a disciple for thirteen years, leads a ministry group and works as an engineer. Listen to how she depends on God's sovereignty:

> I believe that everything has its own time and place to be resolved. I understand that I must hand over my anxieties to God. It's great to know that he is much stronger than I, more intelligent than I, and that I'm not the omnipotent one—he is!

Betina regularly asks God to show her what is most important on her agenda and then trusts God to lead her. She "marvels" at the way God has blessed her, giving her the time, peace and wisdom she needs to meet all the demands of her busy life.

---

[1] Suggestion: do a study of one of the Gospels to see how Jesus deals with interruptions.

This can sound so challenging, even impossible! Can we really please God, fulfill our responsibilities, meet the needs of others and still maintain our own peace—and sanity? Silvia, a thirty-three-year-old single professional has this to say:

> The way I see it, a balanced life is one that is constant emotionally, spiritually, personally and professionally, yet not necessarily a "complete success" in all these areas at any given point. A balanced life means that all the important areas of our lives are directed by God and are successful in terms of what God values—purity, righteousness, peace, joy and constancy, without fear and without guilt.

Did you catch what she said? Balance does not mean perfection. In fact, we will often swing way over to one side and then way over to the other. A balanced life does not mean that everything every day falls into the exact correct proportion. Some days we will emphasize the ministry, other days, our jobs, others, our families, etc. But if during the course of time, we have sought God's strength and guidance in these areas; if we have kept God and his kingdom first; if we have given our best and not neglected the areas of priority in our lives; and if we have demonstrated the fruits of the spirit—love, joy, peace, patience, kindness, goodness, faithfulness, gentleness and self-control (Galatians 5:22–23)—while doing so, we are on the right track to a balanced life.

What will help us achieve a balanced life? A daily planning notebook is useful or a PDA if you are more high-tech. But I believe a true key to the organizational system that we all can master is passion. Jesus had passion for what was most important in life, and as disciples, we are called to follow his example. Like Jesus, we feel our need to stay close to God. We need to pray. We must hunger and thirst for God's word. We depend on our time with God to give us strength. We are compelled by the love of Christ (2 Corinthians 5:14) to study the Bible with people. We believe fervently in God's plan for marriage and thus protect it at all costs. We yearn to be together with our children in heaven, and so we do whatever it takes to help them to be strong spiritually. We love our Christian brothers and sisters, and so we must spend time with them in fellowship or discipleship. These are things that are so important to us, so much a part of us, that we *will* make the time for them and we *won't* let ourselves neglect them.

The bottom line is we will do what we love to do. Let us keep our eyes on Jesus and passionately embrace what Jesus loves. Then we will be able to enjoy the glorious and fulfilling life God has planned for each one of us!

Helpful Time-Saving Hints
From Women in the Saõ Paulo Church

- Keep a running shopping list on the refrigerator so that when market time comes, you just grab your list and go.

- Divide the work with anyone who can help. Even though it doesn't seem like much, a potato already peeled, a few clothes folded and put away does make a difference.

- Be a list lover! Getting the mass of details out of your head and onto a piece of paper helps make it manageable and helps you to visualize solutions.

- Think backward to make sure you plan the time you will need. For example, I must get to church at 7:00 PM, so I need to leave at 6:30 PM, eat by 6:10 PM, start dinner by 5:40 PM, etc.

- Get lots and lots of advice—why reinvent the wheel when others can share their experiences?

- Memorize scriptures about peace and trusting in God.

Group Session Six

Questions

1. After reading chapter 5, "Keep Your Eyes on Jesus," write down what it means to you to keep your eyes on Jesus as you walk through life.

2. Barbara says that "although the joy is set before us, we don't want to wait for it. Like a spoiled child, we stomp our feet and say to God, 'Daddy, I want it now!'" (page 89). When have you recently had this attitude?

3. Consider the flexibility of the Israelites when they were wandering in the desert (pages 91–92). How do you think you would have handled that nomadic lifestyle? What can you learn from the Israelites that will help you live your life in the twenty-first century?

4. Think of an example from your life when you have had to fix your eyes on something in order to keep focused. Be ready to share your example with the group, along with a spiritual application.

Action Item

- Read the account of Peter walking on water in Matthew 14:21-33. Put yourself in Peter's place. What "winds" can cause you to take your focus off Jesus and to feel that you are sinking? Write down the "winds" and then write out a scripture for each one that will help you to focus on Jesus in this particular area of your life. (If you have children, do a devotional in which you act out Peter's walk. Have each person share what the "winds" are for them.)

Meeting Time

1. Share with each other your answers to each of the above questions and discuss.

2. Barbara says, "If my goal is truly to glorify God, I will be more focused on having a joyful heart than a perfect 'finished product,' even if this means sandwiches instead of filet mignon." If time allows, discuss how you can help each other not be so "results oriented."

3. Commit to read chapter 6, "Aware of Your Variables," answer the questions, and do the action items before coming to the next meeting.

4. Pray together.

Remember that fixing our eyes on Jesus means
never taking them off...no matter what's happening.

chapter 6
Aware of Your Variables

6

Linda Brumley
Seattle, USA

A few years ago, as a result of an assignment, I created a picture collage to illustrate what femininity meant to me. I pored over magazines, cutting and pasting images onto a piece of poster board. A little to my surprise (because I had never really analyzed it before), I was not collecting pictures of fashion or hairstyles, but pictures of women in happy activity and relationships. As my project progressed, I realized that in order to accurately depict my own view of femininity, I could not stay neatly within the measured rectangle of my poster board. To me, femininity is a happy life that spills off the edges! This may not fit every woman's idea of what it means to be feminine, but I find that most of the women I know are, indeed, spilling off the edges—some happily and some not.

Let's face it, we are very busy! Some of the activities and responsibilities in our lives are a result of our own choices and some are not. Perhaps on a good day we can balance it all and make forward progress, but then comes "the wind and the waves"—those variables that are sometimes gentle breezes, sometimes gale-force winds and tidal waves threatening to topple and swamp us, just like the boat Jesus and his disciples were in:

> A furious squall came up, and the waves broke over the boat, so that it was nearly swamped. Jesus was in the stern, sleeping on a cushion. The disciples woke him and said to him, "Teacher, don't you care if we drown?" (Mark 4:37–38)

The good news is that, yes, Jesus does care, and he knows just what it takes to calm the storm and help us to stay balanced on our wire:

> He got up, rebuked the wind and said to the waves, "Quiet! Be still!" Then the wind died down and it was completely calm.
> He said to his disciples, "Why are you so afraid? Do you still have no faith?"
> They were terrified and asked each other, "Who is this? Even the wind and the waves obey him!" (Mark 4:39–41)

Jesus has the power and wants us to tap into it with our faith. But Satan passionately wants to destroy us. Unlike most high-wire walkers, we have to deal with the certainty that someone is scheming against us, hoping to make us fall and miss our goal. But "we are not unaware of his schemes" (2 Corinthians 2:11), his plotting.

As we mentioned in chapter 1, a wise wire walker always considers her variables and trusts God to help her with the winds in her life. Often, as I watch other women maintaining their balance in the face of winds that might blow me away, they become my heroes and a source of inspiration that encourages my heart. Let's meet some of them now.

Daily Demands

The busiest women I know are wives and mothers who also have full-time employment. My friend Lynne is such a woman. She's a women's ministry leader whose time-consuming, high-responsibility job spans oceans and continents and requires significant amount of travel. She has a vibrant household, including a wonderful husband and two beautiful, bright children whose interests and activities add to Lynne's already full schedule. Then there are the two rambunctious Border collies, who have demands of their own. Lynne has just recovered from mononucleosis and is in the middle of a move to a new house—definitely a couple of challenging winds.

How does she get it all done? She's a master multi-tasker. She exercises and walks her dogs while having a discipling time with a Christian friend. She cooks two meals at a time, freezing one for later. She groups errands to save miles and time. Her grocery list and her children's schedules are posted on her refrigerator for handy reference. Like the busy woman in Proverbs 31, "she watches over the affairs of her household, and does not eat the bread of idleness."

Lynne regularly self-evaluates, either enjoying a satisfying sense of achievement from a job well done or readjusting when things are not working. She consistently asks for input on her schedule from her husband and friends. She knows which tasks are most appropriate to delegate. She stays sensitive to the unity and romance in her marriage, putting on the brakes to schedule a day alone with her husband or an occasional overnight away.

For Lynne, keeping her balance means protecting her priorities: God, husband, children, church and the unbelievers, in that order. It is easy, when winds come, to feel guilty that one area or another is being neglected. This guilt can cause us to swing like a pendulum to the other extreme to try to compensate for a perceived negligence. Objective input is key at these times, as well as remembering your bedrock commitments. Lynne says,

Keeping your balance is a matter of trusting God. When the wind blows hard from one direction, you have to return to center, rather than overcompensating and getting off balance in the other direction. Sometimes you just have to stop and remember where center is so you can get back to it.

Much of the Christian life is about staying the course, with our priorities firmly in place, trusting God to take care of peripheral issues. (See Matthew 6:25–34 and Philippians 3:7–16).

Fear and Finances

My friend Lena is a single mom who has supported herself and her three sons on her wages as a seamstress. She is very familiar with financial pressures, but her trust in God is amazing. She calmly laughs at me and says that I worry more about her finances than she does! But she is not unaware of Satan's schemes. Neither is she unaware of God's provisions, and she trusts him unfailingly.

Lena does all the sensible, practical things. I have watched her seek advice (Proverbs 15:22), refinance her house (Proverbs 10:4) and take on extra work (Proverbs 13:4)—all with a calm assurance of the blessings of God (Proverbs 10:3). Most recently, I have watched her as her son Phillip, away at college, has found his scholarship inadequate to meet his needs. He lost twenty-five pounds from an already trim frame because his food card did not provide enough meals to keep this star soccer player from burning more calories than he takes in. Lena has remained faithful:

I know God is teaching Phillip valuable lessons. I have to let God do his work. I think about Samuel's mom, Hannah, while Samuel was a child and living with Eli. I think about Daniel's mom when Daniel was taken away to live in a pagan king's court. I think about David's mom when David fought Goliath. God was working powerfully in those young men's lives, and I have to let him work in my son's life, too. I try to be content in every situation and let God lead me through it instead of trying to get around it.

Phillip is doing fine! He has not gained back those lost pounds yet, but he is healthy and he has matured amazingly. He is more grateful and less impulsive than the young man who left home two years ago.

Emotional Equilibrium

Most women are familiar with emotional storms. Satan will either cause or use the adverse events of our lives to try to knock us off our wires. He tries to use these winds to make us lose trust in God or react unrighteously under the stress of our anxiety. From the small winds of hormonal patterns to the heartache of loss or the wearying wind of chronic illness, Satan plots against us.

In 1990, I had the privilege of studying the Bible with a wonderful woman. Since she is now in heaven, I cannot ask her permission to use her story, so I will just call her Audrey. She was a fifty-year-old single woman. Surgery to remove a brain tumor had left her with Obsessive-Compulsive Disorder (OCD). OCD had resulted in many anxiety-ridden distortions in Audrey's thinking, and Bible study was often a struggle for her. I was puzzled as to how to help her and tried to understand her illness better. For example, the arrival of the daily mail was an agonizing challenge for Audrey. Every piece of mail represented a difficult decision for her to make: to discard, file, pay now, pay later, respond or not. This turned Audrey into a hoarder; the clutter and piles in every room of her small house were evidence of her painful indecision about things most of us dismiss in seconds.

One day Audrey arrived for our Bible study happy and hopeful because of an article she had read about another woman with OCD. The article talked about a woman with OCD being told the sky was blue. Her response was panic. She hysterically pleaded that such a statement could not be made! Sometimes the sky is azure, sometimes gray or strewn with white clouds, sometimes it's gold and pink or inky-blue and star-flecked. Audrey said that the article helped her understand that her thinking was irrational and not to be trusted, no matter how strong an emotional response it provoked. She understood better why absolute statements were so emotionally charged for her.

In much the same way that John Nash, Jr., as portrayed in the movie *A Beautiful Mind,* decided to let his intellect conquer his demons, Audrey decided, too. Once Nash understood that he was delusional, he decided not to trust his own perceptions. Similarly, Audrey decided to trust the input of other disciples of Jesus and replace her own anxious thinking with their perspectives instead. Not long after this decision, she confidently made Jesus her Lord and was baptized. Throughout the rest of her life, with the sweet and trusting innocence of a child (Luke 18:16–17), Audrey sought and accepted the Biblical perspective and input offered by other disciples to help override her own uncontrollably strong feelings.

What an inspiration she was to me and many other women whose emotional breezes bore little comparison to her emotional hurricanes. When I know I am feeling extra emotional about an issue, I know it is time for objective input! Audrey's inspiring example left no excuse—if she could do it, we can do it (Jeremiah 17:9–10).

Dreams Destroyed

Our youngest son, Matt, had found the girl of his dreams, and he and Julie were married in 1995. They were a perfect match! Both have a passion for life, outgoing personalities, beautiful singing voices and creative imaginations. Most of all, they both loved God, delighted in leading in the teen ministry together and shared a mutual dream of being on the ministry staff.

But four years later, the winds of illness and disappointment left Matt angry and steeped in secret sin. He lost his trust in God and stopped going to church. Julie was stunned—this was not the man she had married.

In an emotional whirlwind, Julie fought to get her bearings. The dreams with which she had begun her married life were shipwrecked, and she pondered what new dreams she might embrace if Matt never came back to God:

> I didn't want to be a woman who became bitter. I kept thinking of the terrible "What ifs?" Because he had left God, I even wondered if he might leave me and asked myself if I could take it? It was my focus on the character of God and knowing he'd be with me no matter what that convinced me I would be okay. But there was so much anxiety and so much fear inside me. The only thing that got me through was my time with God every morning. I didn't have anything else to hang onto.
>
> Once when I felt I was losing hope, I read Romans 5:3–5, where God explains that perseverance produces character and character produces hope. I realized I had to persevere in faith and love and calmness so God could strengthen my character—because only the strong have hope.

Not knowing whether Matt would ever find his way back to God or not, and yet faithfully hoping that he would, Julie focused on her dreams of being a joyful, grateful daughter to God. She worked harder than ever on her own righteousness in being the best wife she could be to Matt and in using all her talents for God.

A year and a half later, Matt came back to God, and they are once again happily serving him together. None of us may know until heaven how much Julie's sweet faith and perseverance contributed to Matt finding his faith again!

Love Lost

On two occasions in our forty-one years of marriage, Ron, my husband, has faced life-threatening illnesses. It crossed my mind during those times that I might be facing the seemingly devastating wind of widowhood. It was a frightening thing to contemplate, and it has made me take note of other women who have kept their balance in the face of that wind. They will be the women I remember and call on and imitate if I must ever go on without Ron.

I remember being with my special friend Irene shortly after George, her husband of fifty-one years, had died. I was amazed to see her embracing her new life as a single woman with joy and zeal. I recall her saying, "I loved being married to George, but I love my life now, too." Her secret to joy was finding all the new ways that God still planned to use her life—and serving him wholeheartedly. She began leading groups of women whose husbands were not Christians. She called them "Sarah's Daughters," and Irene still says today that they are her favorite ministry. But always seeking a new challenge (at eighty-plus years old!), she has this year started a new group which she calls "Anna's Daughters" for the widows of ministry leaders. It includes widows, young and old, from all over.

My dear friend Cleo is part of that group. She said that one of the hardest things about widowhood for her is making decisions alone, but she said that it was Irene who told her that her husband (also named George) will always disciple and teach her. She has found this to be very true, and she enjoys hearing George's "voice" in this way—as she is still keenly aware of his perspective and counsel whenever she faces a decision. Cleo and George had been married fifty-two years when he died, yet I found her immediately able to joke and laugh. I asked her how she so quickly was able to find her sense of humor in the middle of all the tears, and she said, "It would dishonor George's memory for me not to be able to laugh." Having known George, I was both delighted and comforted by Cleo's attitude.

God never promised us a life without storms. On the contrary, he said we will face them, but we will survive if our house is built on him (Matthew 7:24–29). While I love this promise, I still do not like storms. Rejoicing in "trials of many kinds" (James 1:2–5) is still really hard for me. I pray to avoid storms, and then, in the middle of them, I pray for them to end. I love the story of Jesus calming the storm (Matthew 8:23–27), and I always run to wake him up when storms hit my life! But sometimes God has a greater purpose in the storm than in the calm. The chorus from a favorite song of mine goes like this:

> Sometimes he calms the storm
> With a whispered "peace be still";
> He can settle any sea

But it doesn't mean he will.
Sometimes he holds us close
And lets the wind and waves go wild.
Sometimes he calms the storm—
And other times he calms his child.[1]

It is through the storms that God perfects our balance. God is much more interested in changing our character than in changing our circumstances! Until we get to heaven, strong winds will come unexpectedly from time to time. God will use them to make us stronger, wiser and closer to him if we hang on faithfully to his word and focus straight ahead on the character of Jesus to become like him.

---

[1] Tony Wood and Kevin Stokes, eds., "Sometimes He Calms the Storm," *The Best of Scott Krippayne* (Milwaukee: Hal Leonard, 1995).

Group Session Seven

Questions

1. After reading chapter 6, "Aware of Your Variables," review the life situations that Linda mentioned. Is there one you particularly relate to? Which one and why?

2. Fear of the unknown is a wind that can blow us off our feet, spiritually speaking. What fear most threatens you? What scripture can you focus on to deal with that fear?

3. What dreams have been destroyed in your life—either temporarily or permanently? How has God helped you deal with this variable?

4. How have you gone after having new dreams?

Action Items

- Identify a friend who has gone through a difficult time of some sort, yet has kept her faith. Initiate some time with her to talk about how she weathered the storm without giving up or leaving God.

- Memorize the scripture you identified above to help you deal with your fear.

Meeting Time

1. Share with each other your answers to each of the above questions and discuss.

2. What did you learn from some of the women mentioned in Linda's chapter?

3. Commit to read chapter 7, "Don't Be Afraid to Say No," answer the questions, and do the action item before coming to the next meeting.

4. Pray together.

Remember that we will survive any
storm if our house is built on Jesus.

chapter 7
Don't Be Afraid to Say No

Shelley Metten
Los Angeles, USA

A woman who loves God is a beautiful woman. She embraces the scriptures that teach sacrifice, and her life reflects the heart of a servant. Many orphaned babies live in nurturing Christian homes because a godly woman has wrapped her arms around them. Marriages have been saved as she sacrificially has given of her time to counsel and encourage. Who can count the beautiful dinners, created and hosted by the godly woman wanting to share the gratitude she feels in her heart for God? How many college women were able to avoid substance abuse and its destruction because a friend in one of their classes, a godly woman, taught them about having security in God? And then there is that very young teenage girl who was about to compromise her virginity to win the attention of a guy, but her friend, a godly teen, spoke the truth to her.

A godly woman extends her hands to the needy, puts her arms around the frightened and embraces the lonely. These are her virtues and her dignity. But as with all aspects of nature and God's creation, the physical expressions of our virtues must have boundaries. To be sacrificial is to have the heart of Christ, but it must be motivated by a pure desire to please God and to give back to him out of our gratitude. Therefore, the boundary of sacrifice is a pure heart. If we say yes to please people or to look good, for example, we have crossed the line from sacrifice to worldliness. The outside of the cup has become more important than the inside, as it often did for the religious leaders of Jesus' day:

> "You clean the outside of the cup and dish, but inside they are full of greed and self-indulgence. Blind Pharisee! First clean the inside of the cup and dish, and then the outside also will be clean." (Matthew 23:25–26)

As Christians, the heart behind our responses and actions is the important element. It is not the outside of the cup that God admires. He looks at the heart, what is inside, the why of what we do. Sacrifice from a pure motivation, a cup that is clean on the inside, is a fragrant offering to God and brings him pleasure. The question that we may need to ask ourselves, then, is not, "Should I say no?" but rather, "Why am I saying yes?"

Wrong Motivations Behind Yes

The process of maturing as a Christian is really a slow purification of our hearts, replacing unhealthy motivations with godly ones. There are many old experiences and hurts tucked away in the deep recesses of our hearts. Some are the consequences of the sins of others as they abused us, but most are consequences of the sinful choices we have made. How we respond to this pain has shaped our character and taught us unhealthy patterns of responding to others. Motivations become tainted by both the need for approval and the fear of unpleasant consequences.

However, maybe it was not abuse but neglect that has shaped our patterns. Children raised in homes in which there was very little discipline—or even excessive indulgence—will develop unhealthy ways of responding to life in order to get attention. As Christians, we bring into our new life all these old motivations and response patterns. Therefore, there are many different wrong motivations behind the word "yes," but here are a few examples that are probably familiar to many of us.

Staying Busy

One very common response that springs from a hurtful or abusive past is to extend ourselves beyond our limits, thinking that being busy means we are being spiritual and "good." Conveniently, it also prevents us from slowing down long enough to deal with whatever pain is bubbling just under the surface.

In the world, overachieving is an acceptable way of hiding the pain of insecurity. Our society highly regards women who are successful multi-taskers, and many of us have brought this value system into the kingdom with us.

Then what happens is, these hard-working women are always the first ones asked to serve because they are reliable and consistently say yes. But it's impossible to keep our balance on the high wire of life while crossing it at light speed—as many of us know from experience! The falls will come.

If what we are doing is overachieving our abilities, we are not establishing clear and healthy boundaries motivated by God's grace and love for us. If our motivation is healthy, our limits will also be appropriate. It is each woman's responsibility to look at her own heart. Honesty will slow the overachieving wire walker down because she—

and others—will finally know *why* she is so eager to take on every task that comes her way. She will learn that "it does not, therefore, depend on man's desire or effort, but on God's mercy" (Romans 9:16).

Seeking Approval

A second big pull on our hearts is compulsion—the strong feeling of "I have to." One of the most powerful compulsions is to act in such a way as to receive approval, especially from authority figures. We call this type of woman a "people-pleaser." (This is really a funny expression, however, because deep down, the only person she is trying to please is herself!) It is not difficult to identify the woman who says yes out of a need for approval: if she does not receive the recognition that she is seeking, resentment and bitterness are the unmistakable hallmarks of her heart.

Unfortunately, there are many women who respond out of compulsion and not out of sincere desire. These women feel that they *have* to do something, not that they *want* to do something. In essence, they are making a choice against their will. This is clearly not what God desires, which he made clear through the apostle Paul, teaching here about financial contributions: "Each man should give what he has decided in his heart to give, not reluctantly or under compulsion, for God loves a cheerful giver" (2 Corinthians 9:7).

Perfectionism

God wants us to be surrendered women, not women who are caught up in emotional bondage and fear. We may have hidden fears of disappointing someone or being punished unless we say yes to authority figures. Women raised in homes filled with fighting and angry words learned to be perfectionists in order to keep from being yelled at themselves. Furthermore, if one or both of their parents were addicts, they walked on thin ice, always trying to keep peace in a volatile environment.

These women come into the church with all these fears. If they sense an emotionally charged confrontation about to take place, they will quickly try to be perfect and calm the situation by obeying everything they are told to do. The woman whose life is controlled by this kind of fear is really living a double life, a life of deceit. Who we are on the inside must be the same as who we are on the outside. The only way out of this trap is to become painfully honest and to learn to confront the "threatening" situations. Through discipleship we can help each other to learn how to have a godly response to authority by working through each situation and seeing the truth in it—truth sets us free. (See John 8:32.)

Controlling Others

A fourth impure motive for saying yes has the potential to be the most destructive. This is when a woman wants to serve and take care of people as a means of controlling them or controlling her environment. A contemporary word for this is "codependency." These women serve all the time, and certainly their efforts are appreciated. But when the desire to serve becomes controlling or oversteps the boundaries of healthy giving, the motivation is no longer godly. The people who are the recipients of the controlling behavior feel trapped and manipulated. The controlling woman at first feels energized by the opportunity to take care of someone, but when the controlled person begins to hold firm boundaries, the controlling woman feels deeply hurt by the rejection she feels. Boundaries in relationships are important and Biblical:

> Do nothing out of selfish ambition or vain conceit, but in humility consider others better than yourselves. Each of you should look not only to your own interests, but also to the interests of others. (Philippians 2:3–4)

The codependent woman can find freedom in this passage. It reminds us that it is okay to be concerned about our own interests and needs. God wants to take care of us, but he also does not cross the line. He gets involved as we invite him in. Once the codependent woman realizes that each person has responsibility for him- or herself and that she does not need to feel responsible for someone else's choices and emotions, then she can begin to help herself.

Getting in touch with what motivates us to give and serve is essential to maintaining a healthy, godly spirit in our relationships with one another and with God.

Be in Touch with Your Physical Limitations

Our motivations might be good, yet we still need to carefully evaluate our choices before we say yes or no. As we are wrestling with our motivations, a second problem we can encounter in saying yes is doing so beyond our limitations. At this point, if you know me personally, you are probably wondering why I was asked to write this chapter! But it is always good to consider our weaknesses, and this is certainly one of mine. I do not realize how far I have gone beyond my limitations until I smash into the wall. Then it can take days to get physically and emotionally back on my feet. However, with much study, great input into my life and just a little maturity, my perspectives have changed. What I have come to realize is that, although it is certainly true that our souls will live forever, our bodies are not going to be here long if we do not start taking better care of them.

Rest—Gotta Have It

Many of us became Christians when we were in our twenties. We lived on fast food; six hours of sleep was oversleeping; and we thought taking time out for relaxation was something you did when you were much older. Sadly, many of us are now "much older," and we are beginning to pay the price for unwise decisions we made during our youth. What is even more alarming is the number of young women whose bodies are showing signs of stress at very early ages. Chronic fatigue, fibromyalgia and depression are among the more common problems young Christian woman are experiencing. Even though the causes of these physical and emotional problems in many cases are unknown, one thing we do know is that we need to place clear limitations on our responses to the pressure we feel. If our response to stress doesn't cause these types of diseases, it certainly exacerbates them.

Women's bodies are made differently than men's bodies. In biomedical research, we are just now beginning to fully appreciate how significant the difference might be. For example, it is relatively common for a woman to develop an autoimmune disease like lupus, but it is much less likely for a man to acquire this type of illness. There are also diseases that are more common to men than women. Women are also different in that we have a monthly hormonal cycle that includes daily hormonal gyrations. We need consistent sleep (eight hours is great), and we need to eat a healthy diet to replace blood loss and have the nutrients available for hormone production and tissue repair. Additionally there are changes that take place in our lives that require us to rethink what we are doing. One such time is right after your baby is born. A young mom needs rest so that she can produce adequate milk for her baby. She needs time to bond and nurture the child. If she jumps back into a busy schedule too quickly, her health will be compromised both immediately and in the future. And as we age, our body has different needs that we must respond to so that we can live satisfying lives. Aging is a beautiful process that can be accepted and enjoyed.

Stress Busters

In learning our limitations, probably the most important lesson to learn is how to deal with stress in a way that minimizes its negative effect on our bodies and our minds. Stress over long periods of time wears out our bodies. The systems that are turned on when our bodies perceive a threat or get overworked alter metabolic pathways and brain chemistry. Many of us are stressed so much of the time that we do not realize that we are living in an unhealthy, altered state. When we finally allow ourselves to relax, immediately the tension is released from places like our neck and shoulders. Our digestive system starts working more smoothly with less irritation and bloating. There is even a change in our emotional state and our perspective about our environment.

When we have experienced too much unabated stress, even when we take the opportunity to relax, we can initially feel depressed and depleted of energy because we have overspent our body's reserves. Exhaustion is the result. It will take time for our bodies to replenish the necessary chemicals that have been used up, as well as to restock the energy stores that will annihilate the fatigue. Even chemicals in the brain are affected by stress and exhaustion, and when these are altered, there will be mood changes. On top of all this, fat tends to accumulate around the waist of the overstressed individual, especially in women!

Our Bodies, Ourselves

Setting boundaries begins by becoming aware of how our bodies are responding to everyday life. We have a personal responsibility to draw limits for ourselves. If we are blaming other people or our circumstances for the fact that we are stretched too far and too much is being expected of us, in truth we are blameshifting. It is no one else's responsibility to set limits for us, and therefore, the stress we feel is no one else's fault except our own. Once we take personal responsibility for our choices, we can begin to set limits that help our bodies to relax and heal. The spiritual giant is not the one who is stressed and exhausted! The woman who is balanced in her walk with God will also be balanced in her metabolic processes, mental health and her schedule.

Quality Time with God

Not only is it important to be at peace with our bodies' physical and emotional limitations for health reasons, but also for our relationship with God. God's Spirit cannot have the impact on our lives that God has intended when we, by our own choices, are stressed and burdened. These are hard scenes to imagine when we are living at Mach five with our hair on fire:

> The LORD is my shepherd, I shall not be in want.
> He makes me lie down in green pastures,

> he leads me beside quiet waters,
> > he restores my soul.
> He guides me in paths of righteousness
> > for his name's sake. (Psalm 23:1–3)

> Be still before the LORD and wait patiently for him;
> > do not fret when men succeed in their ways,
> > when they carry out their wicked schemes.
> (Psalm 37:7)

Scripture after scripture teaches that God's desire and direction for us is to find the green pastures and the quiet waters. He knows that we will listen more carefully to him when we are quietly meditating on him. Even with our friends and family, we know how difficult it is to get someone's attention when they are distracted and rushed. Our best conversations happen over tea in the cozy corner of our favorite restaurant or curled up in overstuffed chairs in our best friend's home. With our children, it is at night when we climb onto their bed with them that we get to share those special conversations. How much more important is it to spend quiet time with God? He cherishes the quiet moments with us. Saying yes so often that we no longer have time in our schedule for special conversations with God reveals that we have missed the point.

God wants us to learn to serve *his* way, not the way we have learned in the world:

> But now, by dying to what once bound us, we have been released from the law so that *we serve in the new way of the Spirit,* and not in the old way of the written code. (Romans 7:6, emphasis added)

> Serve wholeheartedly, as if you were serving the Lord, not men. (Ephesians 6:7)

It will take some effort to restudy the Scriptures and rethink what it means to serve God not men, including not serving our own worldly motivations.

In saying all this, though, are there times that life's demands will cause us to overstep some bounds? Yes. This is unavoidable. Times of family stress and sickness will ask more of us than we think we have—physically, emotionally and spiritually. During those times should we think that something unfair is happening to us? No, these times are simply "givens" in anyone's life.

> "Therefore everyone who hears these words of mine and puts them into practice is like a wise man who built his house on the rock. The rain came down, the streams rose, and the winds blew and beat against that house; yet it did not fall, because it had its foundation on the rock." (Matthew 7:24–25)

If our life has been balanced, it is like building on the rock. When the storms come, we may get battered, but we remain standing. Setting healthy limits that provide great times with God builds a life that is emotionally strong. We will not only face the trials, but we will be able to laugh at the ones to come.

When to Say Yes—or No

> "Everything is permissible"—but not everything is beneficial. "Everything is permissible"—but not everything is constructive. Nobody should seek his own good, but the good of others. (1 Corinthians 10:23–24)

There is freedom in Christ, so we can say yes whenever we think it is best. But the Scriptures do admonish us that our choices need to be beneficial to us and to the people influenced by them. With this freedom of choice that God has given us comes responsibility. We are responsible for our motives; therefore we need to examine our hearts and determine why we are saying yes. We need to realize it will take years to sort through all those deep recesses of our hearts. Yet, year after year, layers come off, and we become clearer in our thoughts and in our motivations. We should not overanalyze everything we say, but we must realize, that when we are responding out of a pure heart, we will feel peaceful inside…and peace will show up on the outside as well.

So, when is it acceptable to say no? Whenever we think it is best, for all the same reasons and with the same responsibilities. For some of us, learning to say no is much more difficult than learning to say yes. Having mature Christian women in our lives who can help us sort it all out is the biggest blessing of all. A true friend will look behind the mask and help us admit to what we already know is there. Where else, except in the church, can we find the healing touch of love that can help us to never be afraid to say no?

It is so important that we examine our lives and our responses because others are trying to imitate us and our faith. For example, our own daughters will do what we do because they have been trained by us. My daughter, Jennifer, who is twenty-seven, has tried so hard to do all the things that I do. But her body is different than mine. She just does not have the same stamina I have. Also, her heart is different than mine spiritually. She was raised in a Christian home, and as a result, she is more confident with herself and does not feel the need to overachieve to win approval. She has stretched herself beyond healthy limitations at times because she has wanted to imitate what she sees me doing. Growing up, she would watch me walk in the house from work, prepare dinner (oftentimes with guests coming over), put her and her brother to bed and then stay up late into the night finishing projects for both work and home. Our weekends were often packed.

Through the years as I have watched her pursue her dreams, the differences in our motivations have made me examine my own motivations. We have had some great talks about my past, ways I have overcontrolled situations out of fear and how many times I have extended myself too far because I thought it was the right thing to do. I wanted her to know that my example of doing too much was the wrong example. Now I am learning to say no to myself and to others, and it is important to me that my daughter feels this same freedom. We are learning from each other and Jennifer has become the woman in my life who helps me the most to set healthy, spiritual limits for myself.

Additionally, we have a responsibility to teach the younger women in our churches the right priorities and how to have the kind of lives that are also worthy of imitation. Here is what Paul had to say to his young disciple Timothy:

> Likewise, teach the older women to be reverent in the way they live, not to be slanderers or addicted to much wine, but to teach what is good. Then they can train the younger women to love their husbands and children, to be self-controlled and pure, to be busy at home, to be kind, and to be subject to their husbands, so that no one will malign the word of God. (Titus 2:3–5)

It will help the young women in our churches if we start talking about how we have made our choices and how we would choose differently now. Our example is so important, and we want them to live balanced lives as they raise their families and serve God.

Ultimately, what matters is our heart and how God feels about our heart. As Jesus said,

> "Simply let your 'Yes' be 'Yes,' and your 'No,' 'No'; any-thing beyond this comes from the evil one." (Matthew 5:37)

It is simple: we need to learn to say yes and no out of a pure heart that loves and serves God and his people. We need to make choices like Jesus did by seeking to please God and allow him to order his time and his schedule.[1] Then, like Jesus, we will have the peace that comes from godly motivation.

---

[1] Remember the emphasis of chapter 2, how Jesus made decisions not to please himself and not to please others. He simply prayed daily to respond to God and to please him with all his choices.

Group Session Eight

Questions

1. After reading chapter 7, "Don't Be Afraid to Say No," answer this question: Which of the four wrong motivations behind saying yes are you most tempted to have?

2. How do you reconcile dying to yourself (being sacrificial) and saying no when you really believe it is best? (See the last paragraph of Rose's comments on page 22–23 in chapter 1.)

3. How do you personally discern when to say no?

4. How do you communicate with someone when you feel you must say no to a request? What is important to remember about this communication?

Action Item

- Pray about your motivation when you say yes to requests. Ask God to show you if you are seeking a heavenly reward or an earthly reward. Allow him to purify your heart as you begin to understand your motivations. Be prepared to share with the group what you find.

Meeting Time

1. Share with each other your answers to each of the above questions and discuss.

2. Discuss with each other the importance of not overreacting to this chapter and allowing the "right" to say no to feed your selfishness or laziness.

3. Commit to read chapter 8, "Order in Your World," answer the questions, and do the action items before coming to the next meeting.

4. Pray together.

Remember to let your "Yes" be "Yes" and your "No" be "No,"
but only after giving God your day, your time, your life.

chapter 8
Order in Your World

8

Kitty Chiles
New York City, USA

*I*magine a world where life naturally organized itself. Furniture was always dusted, toys put themselves away, and the laundry was somehow washed, dried, folded, ironed and found its way into closets and drawers. At dinnertime, the menu, complete with recipes, would be posted on the refrigerator, which contained all the necessary ingredients. As you prepare the meal, the dishes find their way into the dishwasher. The timer goes off, and as you pull dinner from the oven, your family simultaneously sits down to a perfectly set table. What a dream! It makes me laugh to think that my special room in God's mansion will be self-cleaning and self-stocked. (How could it be heaven if I have to still be the cleaner and stocker?!)

Well, this may be the world Mary Poppins lives in, but it is not the world we live in. Naturally speaking, "Chaos reigns." Left unattended, our homes and lives become messy and chaotic. The very place that is meant to be a refuge, our home, can become a source of anxiety and unhappiness if we do not work to maintain order. In our offices, as well, if things are disorganized, undisciplined and in disarray, we are not able to be productive and great examples to our bosses and coworkers. Our work lives demand that we maintain an environment that allows us to think, create, respond and do our part.

There is something in all of us, I believe, which wants to make order out of chaos. In *Reflection on the Psalms* C. S. Lewis wrote, "The order of the divine mind, embodied in the divine law, is beautiful. What should a man do but try to reproduce it, so far as possible, in his daily life?"[1] However, while we might desire order, I think we can all agree that maintaining it in our homes and offices can be very challenging. There is so much "in-coming"—friends on the other end of the line, a knee that needs a bandage, the dust flying in the door or an abrupt change in the boss's priorities—that we can often feel as though we want someone to "make the world go away...." But while we are not to be *of* the world, we are *in* the world, and it's not going to go away until Jesus comes again. In the meantime, we are responsible for helping our friends, bandaging that knee, dusting, adjusting and maintaining a balanced and ordered life.

God Loves Order

We can learn so much from each other in this area of maintaining order in our lives. I have had the opportunity to talk with a number of women for whom "ordering" is a strength, and they have some great pointers which I want to share with you. But first, I think it is important that we understand that all the tools in the world will not help your life to be orderly unless you have the mind-set that order is important.

When God created the world, he essentially brought order out of chaos. All through the first chapter of Genesis, God paints the picture of creation as one of ordering. "He separated the light from the darkness," creating days for us to mark time (Genesis 1:4). He "separated the water under the expanse from the water above it," setting apart

---

[1] *Quotable Lewis,* Wayne Martindale and Jerry Root, eds. (Wheaton, Ill.: Tyndale House Publishers, 1989), 463.

the sky (Genesis 1:7). He created vegetation, birds and animals "according to their various kinds" (Genesis 1:11, 12). God created, separated, organized and named, resulting in an order to things that allows for a peaceful working and interaction. Truly, "God is not a God of disorder but of peace" (1 Corinthians 14:33). The incredible order in nature is a constant reminder to us of the ordered nature of God.

Careful Circumspection

I have done a number of studies that have helped me to develop conviction about how I need to think so as to maintain peace and prevent chaos from reigning in my life. Recently I studied about being "circumspect," which *Webster's* defines as being "careful to consider all circumstances and possible consequences." I believe circumspection is a prerequisite to maintaining order in our lives. If we do not consider the consequence of not doing the laundry today, we may wake up tomorrow and realize that little Cindy's cheerleading uniform will not be ready for the tryouts that morning. The result will not be peace! If we are not circumspect, we will have no eggs when we are ready to bake that special birthday cake in the *only* hour we have allotted. Keeping order in our lives demands that we look ahead each day and consider the consequences of our actions—or lack thereof.

Connie, an empty-nester with a very demanding job and schedule, suggests using your time with God each morning to practice being circumspect. She prays and thinks about all that she needs to do that day and organizes her day accordingly. Sara, a single woman working in the teen ministry of the New York church commented, "I usually take five to ten minutes each morning to write out telephone calls I need to make, errands I need to run, tasks I need to accomplish. I also consider how

reflection

best to use the time available to spend with people." We need to give ourselves some time to reflect on what it will take each day to keep our
homes, offices and lives in order.

Dear Prudence

Another word study that helped me to have conviction about my
day was "prudent." The Bible has much to say about being prudent or
being women who govern or discipline ourselves. Keeping order in our
lives requires prudence. Several Proverbs have been helpful in reminding
me that God wants me to be a thoughtful, prepared woman: "A prudent
man gives thought to his steps" (Proverbs 14:15), and "a prudent wife is
from the Lord" (Proverbs 19:14). I don't know exactly how the woman
in Proverbs 31 accomplished all that she did with such apparent ease
and grace, but I think she must have been circumspect and prudent. I
think she must have been careful to weigh the circumstances of her life
each day and the consequences of her actions. She had to be a woman
who disciplined herself to do what needed to be done in spite of how she
felt. I picture her thinking through her day the night before and then
again the next morning. I think she probably made many preparations
the night before to ensure that her day would go smoothly and that all
the needs of her family, friends and employees would be met. She had
to always be looking ahead and working to conform her feelings to her
plan in order to accomplish as much as she did.

A Jesus Day

A number of years ago, I came to the realization that many of my
days did not look like Jesus' days. I always had a to-do list with all kinds
of action items. But I realized that I tended to attack the nonpeople

items first, rationalizing that I would get the tasks out of the way first. This was true at the office as well as at home. Yet, by the end of the day, I still had more work at the office, more floors to mop *and* many calls I had not made, invitations I had not extended, and things unsaid that I needed to say. I made a decision to let the people's needs take higher precedence for me. I decided that when God presented the needs of others to me, I should attend to them more quickly. I had to trust him to work things out so that I could get everything else on my to-do list done. It has been amazing to watch God work out my days as I learn to trust him with my schedule. Now I get a lot more of *his* work done, and my nonpeople items have rarely suffered.

Approaches to Scheduling

Once you have a conviction about the need to be ordered in your home and office, there are so many practical ways to organize your life. As I age, I am more and more aware of my need to write down everything! But even as a young working mother, I found a planning notebook to be invaluable.

Prepared with a Planner

I am always amazed when I meet someone who actually lives life without an organizer. I want to know how they could possibly know what to do on any given day and how they could do without this oh-so-essential tool of order. Do they have friends they need to meet somewhere? How will they remember? Do they have a butler who provides for their every need? I don't have a clue how to help myself without obeying the cardinal rule of writing everything down—and I mean everything! I looked at two random days in my Day-Timer and made a list of the types of things I had noted: plan discipling times; HOPE staff meeting at 10:00 AM; call accountant regarding taxes and college scholarship form; schedule adoption workshop; dentist appointment at 5:00 PM; send care packages to Somalia team; buy birthday gift for Heidi; pay credit card bill; follow-up with Cindy and Jennifer (neighbors) about Bible Talk; and more.

My planner is my constant companion. I call it "my life" because, in many ways, this is exactly what it is. I really cannot make a decision without consulting it. When my husband and I sit down to make plans, we make sure we both have our planners (my Day-Timer and his Palm Pilot! He is trying to get me into this millennium, but I'm just an old fashioned pen-and-paper girl.) Whatever our method, it does not matter, as long as we have one and hold to documenting our to-dos and any changes in our schedules every day.

planner time

Locking in the Essentials

Once we have planners, our second step is to put things in them! We have found in our family and formerly with our business, and now with the HOPE work, if we do not take the initiative and plan, life will take over. We have to be responsible and lock in the important pieces of our lives as disciples of Jesus. This will not happen well if we are always doing it on the fly. For example, the weeks when Bud and I sit down, talk, agree and make plans are markedly different from the weeks when we do not. We accomplish more, we are more prepared and we have fewer communication "bumps."

Melanie, a married mother of a toddler, a preteen and a special-needs teen, stressed the importance of "asking for input on my decision-making, especially from my husband. He knows me better than anyone else and can really help me not to get out of focus." If you are single, get input on your schedule from mature Christian friends, and if you live with roommates, make sure you have a time of coordinating your schedules for the week. If you are married, lock in a weekly planning time with your spouse, and if you are someone's boss, help things to go well at work by making plans week by week.

Post-It!

The next "love of my life" in maintaining orderliness are the wonderful little Post-It notes. Yes, you've got it—the little yellow ones. They come in very handy when you want to remember something early in the morning, like a dentist appointment you really would rather forget. I just stick a note on the medicine cabinet so I will see it first thing. (Then if I don't remember, you'll all know that I didn't brush my teeth!)

Multi-tasking

A technique that has helped me to accomplish more in a given period of time is to group things I need to get done. For example, I make calls on my cell phone (safely) during my commute time. I take a friend shopping. My friend Pat uses her travel time on airplanes to write postcards to friends all over the world. Lynette, a single working mother of three girls in Newark, New Jersey, has a great example of grouping responsibilities: "We have a 'teacher appreciation night' at our house for each of my children. I get to know the teacher who is with them all day; I get to share my life and family; my girls feel my concern about their life; and they get a boost in their confidence at school."

Time-Saving Ideas

- If you have access to a computer and are at all technologically inclined, e-mail is a wonderful tool for quick communication. When you do not have the time to get into a longer conversation, I recommend avoiding the telephone. As disciples and women, we are bent toward the more lengthy talks. There is absolutely a time and place for those great talks, but they can be a distraction at times when you need to focus and accomplish a lot. E-mail allows you to send out communication without necessarily immediately receiving. A warning though: e-mail can also suck us in! Watch out for the group messages with all the funny/sad stories, which are fine, but only when you have a lot of time and Kleenexes!

- The women whom I spoke with all mentioned how much it helps them to keep up with a little housework each day. Letting things pile up, like the laundry and other housekeeping chores can leave us with an overwhelming mess when we stop to tackle it. I go to the laundry room almost every morning when I first get up to put in a load of wash. Even if I don't get back until the next morning, at least one load is in progress. Yet, it is helpful to have a set time or day when you do certain chores in order to avoid the dangers of procrastination.

- Meal planning is not one of my favorite pastimes but it really is worth the effort. There's something very satisfying about knowing what I am going to prepare each night and having the ingredients to accomplish it. It makes me feel like a better wife and mother. If menus are not your strength, get a "whiz in the kitchen" to help you. One Christmas, I begged my friend Deb to copy her menus for me instead of buying me a gift. As usual, Deb did far more by preparing meal plans and recipes for me and putting it all in a wonderful little book. If she gets a jewel in her crown for each time I have pulled that little book out, she'll have trouble holding up her head while walking around in heaven!

- Another handy meal tool that a good friend of mine discovered was a grocery list on the Internet. She cut and pasted it into a file on her computer and customized it according to the items that she regularly purchases. So, I came up with a grocery list of my own. It has helped me tremendously not to forget certain items that I need. It makes me feel so efficient to see it all nice and typed up. My old method of writing items on the back of any stray piece of paper and then trying to find them all was definitely not very efficient.

- If you are like me and have a tendency to take on too much, then learning how to include others in helping can be a lifesaving skill. We know that the church is compared to a physical body in which God intends that all the parts have a role in accomplishing all he has given us to do. Including others in helping to accomplish all we have been given is a great way to help everyone to feel useful and to build relationships.

  This was a difficult lesson for me to learn when I became a Christian. God humbled me and helped me to see how much I needed to depend on others through an unusual circumstance. Because of a difficult pregnancy, I was forced to stay in bed for six months. Since I was allowed up for only five minutes each day and had a toddler running around the house, I needed to depend on women in the church for everything. At first I felt very awkward and very indebted to them, but their generosity and reassurances taught me the lesson of a lifetime. God wanted me to understand that he had placed many loving people in my life to help me in all that he had given me to do. When Katie was born, she had many "mothers" who had helped me to have a safe and full-term pregnancy.

Annihilate Procrastination

One final word of advice in maintaining order in your life is *do not procrastinate!* Take that junk on the stairs up *this* time, as there will be more junk there the next time you go up. Go to the dentist when they call to remind you. If you don't, you may end up going in for a root canal that takes a lot more time! Write the chapter for the DPI book today, because tomorrow you may have to mop up the water in your basement from the washing machine hose that broke. (True story!)

I'm really glad that the next chapter after this one is about having fun because I know that all this probably does not sound very fun. But the truth is that you will be more able to relax and enjoy down time if you do not have the pressures of a disorganized life on your back.

Whatever comes your way, I pray that you will stop long enough to embrace an orderliness that will help you to be more at peace and more able to balance this wonderful life that God has given each one of us.

Editor's note: For more input on having an orderly home, see "Order in Your Home" in the Other Helps section, beginning on page 188.

Last Five and First Five

A Web site on organization suggested that you have a "First Five and Last Five" (5/5) list—the ten things you do each day, without fail. The Last Five are done before going to bed, and the First Five are done in the morning.

If you do your 5/5 faithfully, your house will be relatively neat even if you haven't done major cleaning. You won't be embarrassed if someone stops by, and you will have a basic sense of order in your day. But for it to work, you have to make a commitment! Here are a couple of examples of a 5/5 list.

Last Five

Load dishwasher and run if full

Get gym bag organized for next morning

Sort out dirty clothes to be ready to go into washer early next morning

Pick up den area

Make list of things to do for next day and get organized about schedule

First Five

Put clothes into washer

Unload dishwasher if clean and reload

Make bed

Wipe down bathroom after showering and getting ready

Transfer clothes to dryer and put another load into washer

Last Five

Put dishes up and start dishwasher

Clear off and wipe counter top

Put load in washer

Straighten up living room

Put clothes in closet

First Five

Walk the dog

Unload dishwasher

Put breakfast dishes in dishwasher

Wipe kitchen sink and counter

Put clothes in dryer

Cardinal Rule of Upkeep

If you see something that needs to be done and it would only take 30 seconds to do it, do it now!

Group Session Nine

Questions

1. After reading chapter 8, "Order in Your World," answer this question: What new conviction about having order in your life did you formulate?

2. Naturally speaking, on a scale of 1 to 10, how organized are you? If you tend toward "10," how well do you handle interruptions to your schedule? If you tend toward "1," how do you respond to the need to be more organized?

3. Come up with your own Last Five and First Five (5/5) list.

Action Items

- If you do not have a daily habit of thinking through your schedule before going into your day, change and do this each day until your next group meeting. Also put your 5/5 list into practice daily. Be ready to share with the group whether this is helpful to you or not.

- Choose one person whom you believe is exceptionally well organized. Interview her, asking her to share her "secrets" to organization.

Meeting Time

1. Share with each other your answers to each of the above questions and discuss.

2. Consider the following statements:

> It is not possible to live a balanced life unless we live a somewhat organized life.
> It is possible to live an organized life and not live a balanced life.

Discuss whether each statement is true or false, and give reasons for your answer.

3. Commit to read chapter 9, "Don't Forget to Have Fun," answer the questions, and do the action items before coming to the next meeting.

4. Pray together.

Remember that we serve an ordered God,
and we should desire to reflect that order in our lives.

chapter 9
Don't Forget to Have Fun!

Sally Hooper
Dallas, USA

She is clothed with strength and dignity;
    she can laugh at the days to come.
She speaks with wisdom,
    and faithful instruction is on her tongue.

Proverbs 31:25–26

*T*he famous Proverbs 31 woman balances a home, husband, children and servants, while she makes clothes, goes across town for her groceries, buys land, plants a garden, earns extra money, serves the poor, decorates her home, supplies a boutique, teaches and has a great relationship with God. In spite of not getting much sleep, she still manages to maintain her joy and "laughs at the days to come." Surely this woman had days when the market was out of the item she wanted to have for dinner, her servants were sick and did not show up, her garden wilted, or her quiet time was not in the "awesome" category. Yet those occasional occurrences did not dampen her spirit; she could still "laugh at the days to come."

    There have been times when I have let myself get too busy, so that even fun times seemed like a chore. This was never how God meant life to be. In John 10:10 Jesus said he came to bring life to the full. This does not mean just grinding along, trying to stay one step ahead of all our pressing responsibilities. We all need times of rejuvenation and refreshment, even in the midst of the other things we must accomplish. Fun and laughter are from God and are necessary for living healthy lives, both physically and mentally.

God created us with a sense of humor and the ability to laugh. He even made laughter good for our health: it exercises the cardiovascular system by raising and lowering the heart rate and blood pressure; improves coordination of brain functions, enhancing alertness and memory; lifts depression; reduces stress; brings pain relief; aids ventilation and clears mucus in the respiratory system; increases blood oxygen by bringing in fresh air; and strengthens internal muscles by tightening and releasing them. Laughter is one of the body's safety valves—a counter-balance to tension.

So many times over the years, I have caught myself just running from one obligation to the next and gradually losing my joy. Finally, I figured out that I must have fun, refreshing times with people I love or else I start to get negative and critical. The trap I can fall into is feeling guilty about having fun if I do not have everything done—and of course, I never have absolutely everything done. I have had to get to know myself and realize I cannot lead well, serve well, love well or be effective in sharing my faith if I am not having fun, relaxing times with the people God has put in my life.

Fun Is a Magnet

Fun breaks down barriers and is like a magnet that attracts others to us and vice versa. Many of our friends have become Christians after first experiencing a dinner at the Hooper house. Jeff and Laura came to a "stuffed potato" party several years ago. As usual, when I take a foil-wrapped potato from the oven, I throw it on the kitchen counter several times to make the inside soft and fluffy. That evening, I had help from a 6'2" brother. As he threw a potato on the counter, it exploded, covering the kitchen—and especially Laura's hair—with soft, sticky, potato particles! After the initial shock, we all (including Laura) enjoyed a good laugh as we picked tiny pieces of potato from her hair. Jeff and Laura connected with all of us that night and within weeks, became disciples of Jesus. They even later accompanied us to Russia for the marriage of our older son, Dave.

Repentance Is Essential

However, we cannot just make the decision to schedule in fun and expect the time to be great. Sometimes there are sins and other issues in our hearts that can steal our joy. Then no matter how fun our activities are, we will never feel refreshed. Alicia, a woman I admire in the Dallas church, sees her need to repent quickly and not just gloss over things in her heart that require change. She says,

> I have learned that repentance is refreshing and a source of joy. The quicker I repent, the sooner I can experience the blessings God has in store for me. I no longer have to be on the up and down roller coaster ride. There is also a great benefit in discipling. It's wonderful to have Christian friends in my life that can help when my life gets out of balance. I can see their example and imitate their spirit.

I think this kind of heart is a real key to how she manages to accomplish so much. Alicia is the mother of three small, active sons. She and her husband, Fred, a dentist and deacon for the church, are in the process of adopting a baby girl from China. "We keep the fun in our home by first keeping our focus on God, then each other, and then the children," says Alicia. "Fred and I go on dates, play games together, and have weekends away every few months. We enjoy reaching out to our friends and neighbors by going to the park and having friends over for dinner and games. I have learned to get the important things done first, so that I can enjoy these special times."

Attitude Is Everything

Lisa is a single mom with a preteen daughter. She has to balance being a mom with being the best she can be in the workplace, but she has conviction about still making life fun for herself and her daughter. She says that attitude is everything. To keep things balanced and happy in her household, Lisa gets Mandy to bed at a reasonable hour, and then she has some quiet, wind-down time herself before she goes to bed. She uses time on the weekends to plan meals for the week, so she will have more time listening to and playing with her daughter. She says, "Little surprises are a lot of fun for us. Spontaneous things like a late night movie, or a long drive out of the city give us great bonding time and help Mandy to feel special. Sometimes picnics in the park with friends or just plain goofing around are lots of fun."

Because her schedule is so full, she has learned to say no to some additional activities. "It is hard, but I must realize that I'm not the only person God put on the earth to meet needs. When I say no, someone else gets the opportunity to say yes."

Still, with all her responsibilities Lisa can become too serious and has to watch herself. "I get lots of advice. I want to make sure that Mandy has a successful and happy teen experience. I know things are getting out of balance when I forget to check my voice mail messages and my car gets messy. Then I know I must get back to the basics."

Deciding to have a positive attitude can make a huge difference in our lives and the impact we have on others. The positive attitude of Hazel, another friend of mine, always stands out to me. She does not make excuses, and I have never heard her complain. Yet, I have heard some of the younger women complain because they cannot keep up with her! She is one of our much-admired older women in the church. She always seems to be so calm, giving and full of joy. Her secret for having fun is to "always be involved with other Christians, going places and doing things." Because of her joyful, giving attitude she helps many people.

Celebrate! Celebrate!

Practically, how do we learn to work more special, fun times into our lives? One way is to look for things to celebrate. There is always something: birthdays, anniversaries, baptisms, report cards, lost baby teeth, potty training, raises, good conduct in Bible classes, the first day of school, the last day of school, holidays and more. There are many things we can celebrate if we think about it and plan ahead. God's children in the Old Testament had many celebrations and traditions they enjoyed.

Create Memories

Recently, my husband and I, with our daughter Leigh Anne and her family, were watching some old home movies taken mostly on family vacations. After laughing hysterically at her Dad's long sideburns and my "stylish '70s clothes," she commented, "Boy, we visited a lot of fun places growing up!" Fun times build memories, and memories build families.

Sometimes it takes planning and perseverance to have fun. And then we may not appreciate all of the fun until later. On most of our memory-making trips, we camped with our three children in a tent. We survived flies the size of bumblebees, hailstorms, lightning storms, floods, stomach viruses, aching backs, bathroom trips in the middle of the night, ants in our food, 104-degree days and more. But these are not what we all remember the most. We remember being together, breakfast in the open air, hiking trips, meeting new people, swimming in the ocean, museums, Disney World, Williamsburg.... I remember the great talks with each other that took place because we were together and in a different location. Looking back, we can have even more fun, laughing as we remember the "plagues" of those trips.

One of the many fun traditions in our family happens on Christmas Eve. It started because our children had a hard time going to sleep on that magical night. I made gingerbread cookies and everyone in the family decorated one and told a story about their cookie. Most of those cookies met a horrible fate (they got eaten), but the fun and the memories around the kitchen table were priceless. Over the years we have invited family and friends to enjoy our tradition. One year we had forty-five people making gingerbread cookies! It was a long night as each one told his or her story about the mishaps of their cookie.

Our daughter was on the church planting to Moscow, and on Christmas Eve one year, she phoned to say that she had introduced our family cookie-making to the Moscow church. They were having a blast making their cookies. Great, fun memories can be passed on from generation to generation—even country to country.

Our youngest son, Steve, can remember with incredible accuracy, times, places and events. He encourages us often with the fun memories of his childhood. He recently took his wife, Trish, to visit Irmo, South Carolina, where he grew up. They actually took a tour of our old house, and he shared with her the special times we had there.

Home—A Special Place

Last but not least, don't forget to have daily fun with your family. A favorite time at our house was dinnertime. Everyone excitedly told about his or her day. There were two rules:

1. Only positive topics could be talked about.
2. No phone calls would be answered during dinner.

Every now and then, there would even be a spontaneous food fight—usually started by our son Dave. With today's lifestyle, we have to protect the dinner hour. It builds precious memories for the future. Even though Bill and I are now empty nesters, we still make sure that dinner is a special time. There are many other families in the kingdom who can share our table as well, and our own intimate dinners for two are very enjoyable.

Two other couples who seem to have reached a balance in their lives and continue to grow in their joy are Steve and Beverly, and Ron and Randi. Beverly is naturally fun, but even she has to make sure she plans fun times for the family or else they do not happen:

With two teenage children, keeping the priorities straight is a "must." Everyone in our family is very busy. Planning fun times and asking for advice are absolute necessities. Special family nights, dates with my husband, and hospitality need to be planned on a regular basis with everyone involved committed to it.

Randi and her husband, Ron, are now empty nesters, but because of their joyful spirits and hearts to give, God is using them to help so many other Christians. When you enter their home, Randi makes you feel very special. Nothing is too good for her guests. It is obvious she enjoys using her home to entertain. They also have learned that fun is a necessary element in restoring someone spiritually. Instead of slowing down now that their children are grown, they are using their increased flexibility to befriend other Christians by having more fun, bonding times with them.

The writer of Proverbs says, "A cheerful heart is good medicine." As disciples of Jesus, we can have an encouraging effect on those around us as we apply such medicine to their hearts and lives.

A fun, light-hearted spirit is a gift from God. This is why as Christian women we can relax and enjoy those around us in spite of a busy schedule and uncompleted tasks. God wants us to have joyful hearts so we can live life to the full and laugh at the days to come.

Group Session Ten

Questions

1. After reading chapter 9, "Don't Forget to Have Fun," ask yourself this question: Am I a joy to be around?

2. You may or may not be naturally witty or funny, but you can still have fun and be a joy to others. Is there anything that blocks you from having fun?

3. What changes do you need to make in your life in order to be a more fun person?

Action Items

- Talk with your family (or roommates or close friends if you are single) about a fun activity you can do together. Then do it!

- Ask your family or friends if they see you as a person who knows how to relax and have fun. Ask their input on how you might "do better" at having fun.

Meeting Time

1. Share with each other your answers to each of the above questions and discuss.

2. Share a special family tradition from your own life.

3. Set a time to watch a funny movie together and just have a great time!

4. Commit to read chapter 10, "Trust in God's Grace," answer the questions, and do the action items before coming to the next meeting.

5. Pray together.

Remember that God made us with the ability to laugh.
If we don't exercise it, we lose a great gift.

chapter 10
Trust in God's Grace

10

Kay S. McKean
Boston, USA

*H*ere I am, poised with both feet on the high wire. My focal point is Jesus Christ. I do not look down at the ground or around at the crowds, but I keep my eyes on him. I carry the pole in my hands, determined to make my center of gravity my relationship with God. I am aware of the variables, so as to avoid being thrown off the wire by the winds around me. One foot in front of the other, again, again, again. I am making progress! It's an exhilarating feeling to be walking on this wire, leaving the past behind and straining toward what is ahead.

On my next step, one foot reaches out to feel the wire beneath it. Suddenly that foot misjudges and slips off. The wire wobbles. My pole lurches to one side as I try to catch my balance. I waver on one foot, desperate to regain control. Try as I might to stop it, the one foot on the wire, with toes frantically curling to hold on, begins to slide. My momentum is lost, and my body is falling. I fling my hands out to break my fall. Down, down, down I fall, seeing the horror in the eyes of the crowd, hearing their gasps. My fear, shame, guilt and regret flash before me, and I anticipate the hard slam of my body against concrete.

Suddenly I feel a softness, like a cloud, enveloping me. The force of my fall is broken by the net that was beneath the wire all along.

It bounces me, slowly bringing my body to a stop on its woven threads. As I lay in the net, I am incredibly grateful! I have slipped and fallen, but I am not ruined. Only one decision remains between me and my future. Do I climb down from the net, looking no more at the high wire, leaving the daring walk forever, after having fallen so far? Or do I climb up the ladder, take up my pole once again and resume my walk?

This book is about finding balance, about taking the daring walk through our tumultuous world with Jesus as our focus, our Savior and our Lord. We have been given, in the preceding chapters, practical insights that inspire, challenge and motivate us to live in a way that is both pleasing to God and possible for us. Yet even if we took every single piece of advice on every page of this book, we all have the same fatal flaw, the flaw that will knock us off the wire and onto our backs in a moment, in the twinkling of an eye: sin. But, yes, the net will catch each one of us—young and old, married and single, healthy and disabled, poor and rich. We are all sinners who could not even begin the walk without God's grace, and we are sinners who desperately need the net, the net of God's grace. Thankfully that grace is there at the beginning, in the middle and at the end. No wonder Paul would write, "Be strong in the grace that is in Christ Jesus" (2 Timothy 2:1).

Grace Forgives Us

> As for you, you were dead in your transgressions and sins, in which you used to live when you followed the ways of the world.... But because of his great love for us, God, who is rich in mercy, made us alive with Christ even when we were

dead in our transgressions—it is by grace you have been saved. (Ephesians 2:1–2, 5)

I am amazed to remember the grace that God gave me when I first began my walk across the wire. I had not been searching for God, nor was I searching for a noble life or trying to make a positive difference in this world. My journey was an aimless meandering, going the way that would please me the best, and that way led me to promiscuity, drunkenness, deceit and selfishness. Amazingly, God sought me out, turned me around, and put me on the high wire. I am reminded of 1 John 4:10: "This is love: not that we loved God, but that he loved us and sent his Son as an atoning sacrifice for our sins." It was strictly God's grace that enabled me to begin my Christian walk. His love lured me into loving him back and made me yearn for a relationship with him.

Each of us can look back to our beginning steps on our journey with God and remember that no matter who we were or where we came from, God accepted us freely and completely. Yet his forgiveness of our sins at our baptism was only a prelude to the grace he would bestow on us as we continued on our way.

While many of us can passionately recall the forgiveness of our sins when we first became Christians, the challenge to accept God's grace in the here and now can be difficult. We can be tempted to believe that God had had enough grace to forgive us for all the things we did before we knew him, but that he does not have enough grace to cover over the sins of today. This way of thinking is incredibly damaging to us and to those around us. It causes our lives to become off balance, and we walk across the wire in fear, hoping to be perfect in our performance and yet knowing we cannot be. Then when we fail, we pretend it did not happen and are defensive instead of owning up to the fact that we still need a savior. We can also become critical of other Christians who disappoint us, not accepting that God's grace is a safety net for them as well. Or sometimes after a fall, we can become discouraged and faithless about ever walking the wire again.

The solution? For me, the key is remembering that God desires to forgive me! He knows that I am a weak, fragile creature; "he remembers that we are dust" (Psalm 103:14). He set up a plan of salvation that we could not have dreamed of, just so that we could have his forgiveness. Just as he every day gives me the air I breathe and the food I eat so that I can live and thrive on this earth, he also gives me his grace.

The off-balance view of grace that many Christians live with is actually a reaction to the cheap grace we see in much of the religious world around us: people doing whatever they want because "God will forgive everything in the end." We do not want to take God's grace for granted, so we go to the other extreme. Therefore, we teach and talk about what grace is not—taking sin lightly—instead of allowing ourselves to enjoy what it truly is. We tilt our "balancing pole" the other way, believing we have to be perfect to do God's grace justice.

God's grace can and will deal with our sin. It also can and will deal with our frailties and weaknesses. We are "jars of clay" that can be put to great use. And we don't have to be the best, the brightest or the biggest jar to be valuable to God. We just need to be willing. In fact, Paul tells us that his "power is made perfect in weakness" (2 Corinthians 12:9). It saddens me to think of women who feel insignificant in God's church because of life challenges like ill health, financial woes or family problems. These are women who can show us God's grace in its fullness because they must rely on him all the more!

My friend Penny, who suffers from severe diabetes, has learned to rely on God's grace. "Grace helps me to accept that I am not perfect," she says. "I recognize that I have physical limitations and have learned to let go and trust in God." We all have limitations! There is no shame in that! If this is how God himself sees us, why not accept it ourselves? We must allow ourselves (and others) the freedom to acknowledge that we are human beings with hurts, fears and needs. In spite of these things, and perhaps because of them, God can draw us to him and help us to live lives that bring him glory. The longer we feel that we have to perform a certain way or behave a certain way or accomplish a certain thing to receive God's acceptance, the longer we are living unbalanced lives.

Listen to Jesus' description of people who were not accepting of God's grace: "harassed and helpless," "anxious and troubled," "weary and burdened" (Matthew 9:26, Luke 10:41 ASV, Matthew 11:28). These words were indicators of people who were trying hard to do right, live right, follow rules, behave properly. But their efforts left them empty. I know that I have fit into those categories when I have been trying to be a "super-Christian," not wanting to admit failure or needs. Perhaps this kind of thinking is really doubting what the Bible says, as if it is too good to be true. Can we really believe that God is so understanding and compassionate?

Maureen, a divorcée in her mid-30s, has decided to do a thorough study of the subject of grace. One of the things she is learning is the incredible fact that "there is nothing I can do that makes God love me less. Even more amazing, there is nothing I can do to make God love me more!" My daughter, Summer, describes grace this way: "He died for who I am, not for what I do." Accepting God's grace is not just accepting his forgiveness, which is invaluable, but also accepting that we can never earn God's love or favor—it is freely given.

Grace Trains Us

> For the grace of God that brings salvation has appeared to all men. It teaches us to say "No" to ungodliness and worldly passions, and to live self-controlled, upright, and godly lives in this present age, while we wait for the blessed hope—the glorious appearing of our great God and Savior, Jesus Christ, who gave himself for us to redeem us from all wickedness and to purify for himself a people that are his very own, eager to do what is good. (Titus 2:11–14)

I am very grateful for the "safety net" of grace. I know where I would be without it. However, I also know that God's desire for me is to continually get back up on that wire! To stay in the net is to abuse it. God's gift of grace is forever helping me to continue my walk. In fact, after every fall it is Jesus himself who pulls me up and steadies me on the wire. He also helps me learn from my falls in the past, thus hopefully not making the same mistakes again and again.

I can say no to lust because God's grace has shown me the problems it leads to. I can say no to gossip because God's grace has revealed the hurts I have caused in the past by indulging in it. I can say no to sinful anger because I remember the tears that it brought to someone I love. I can say no to bitterness because my gracious God has made it clear that I am mostly hurting myself.

I can also say yes to living a godly life. It is truly, absolutely, positively only God who enables me to do this. I know myself well enough to know where I would be, right now, today, without his love and mercy. I am not talking about where I would be if I had not become a Christian. That thought in itself is quite scary! No, I am talking about where Kay, the Christian woman, the "women's ministry leader," would be without God's grace on a daily basis. It is God who helps me to do what is right. It is God's love that touches me when I am hard and angry. It is God's mercy that enables me to forgive someone who hurts me. It is God's righteousness that reminds me to be pure. It is laughable to me to think that I could be anything useful to God without his grace. Anytime I am tempted to be self-righteous, I remember who I really am, without the grace of God.

When Summer was just five years old, she took the bus home from school for the first time. She was accustomed to children and grown-ups who were good, kind people because of those she knew at church, her friends and extended family and those in her preschool. This bus trip opened her eyes because there were "big kids" on the bus who were swearing, yelling, talking back to the bus driver and disobeying the rules. Even the adult in the picture, the bus driver, was behaving poorly by yelling back and cursing. As Summer got off the bus and we walked home, she told me how bad it was. I realized that she was at a point when she would decide how to view the world around her. I remember telling her, "Summer, you have been around so many good people, but you must remember that they were trying to be good because they know how good God is. Now you are surrounded by some people who don't know this. You can't look down on them or think less of them, but try to show them how good God is and how much he loves them. Maybe that will help them to change." As my children grew up, I tried to keep reminding them—and myself—that we are not better than others, but that the gift of grace is teaching us to live good lives. And we have the opportunity to help others to see God's grace so that they can change, too.

The only way to live a truly balanced life is to remember how much we need the grace of God. When we think we are "better" or that we are good in and of ourselves, our balancing pole will begin to teeter, the wire will shake and we will fall. On the other hand, if we acknowledge our need, then God himself will guide us across that wire, all the way to the end.

One of my favorite parables is about the Pharisee and the tax collector (Luke 18:9–14). Interestingly, Jesus told this parable to "some who were confident of their own righteousness and looked down on everybody else" (Luke 18:9). Jesus then compares the two men, describing the Pharisee as boasting in all he does, while the tax collector humbly acknowledges his sinfulness before God and begs for mercy. But the best news is at the end, when Jesus says, "I tell you that this man [the tax collector]…went home justified before God" (Luke 18:14).

Grace Gives Us Confidence

When I see the challenges of walking across that wire, and I feel the wind around me, and I recognize my own frailties, how then can I walk with confidence and assurance? Because Jesus promises that I am "justified before God." This conviction is what makes me able to continue to take steps, even when I have fallen in the past or fear falling in the future. My walk will not be perfect. I will not always have a completely functional family, flawless relationships or a fabulously ordered home. There will be times when a friend is mad at me, my laundry is piling up, the phone calls were not made, and there is no food in the refrigerator. But I can still be "justified before God."

Years ago, I was studying passages in the Bible in order to grow in my confidence. I particularly remember studying Hebrews 4:16, which tells us to "approach the throne of grace with confidence" and Hebrews 10:19, which says that "we have confidence to enter the Most Holy Place." I read those scriptures over and over again, along with similar passages, trying to muster up this "confidence" that God was speaking about. I tried to convince myself to feel more confident and to talk myself into feeling stronger. My insecurity and my awareness of my weaknesses made it very challenging, and the confident feelings were hard to come by. Finally I stopped looking at the verses as they stood alone, and looked at the context of the passages (always a good thing to do!). Every scripture surrounding those verses had to do with Jesus: his blood, his forgiveness of sins, his sacrifice. I realized that I was looking at confidence as the goal, instead of looking at Jesus as the goal. As I changed my "focal point" to Jesus, my confidence grew, because I was depending on him instead of depending on myself or my feelings. I believe that this is true for any change that I need to make in my life, whether I am striving to grow in joy, gentleness, patience or love. These are all qualities that Jesus embodies, and when I am desiring above all else to be his friend and to walk with him, it is inevitable that I will grow in those godly, wonderful characteristics.

Fabienne serves in the ministry in the church in Paris, France. She is a beautiful, vivacious, outgoing woman, and you would never dream that she struggled with having confidence. Yet she has stated that she relied on her outward qualities to make up for her inner shyness and fear. Fabienne had to wrestle with God and gain her confidence from her relationship with him. I respect her so much for her prayers, her humility and her willingness to grow and change in order to obey God.

She attributes it all to God's grace in her life. She told me, "Understanding God's grace helps me to feel at peace with my Creator, and that balances everything out—the good and the bad. Grace keeps my mind focused on God's qualities and not on my sinful nature."

'I'm at the End of My Rope'

Normally when we hear the phrase, "I'm at the end of my rope," we think of someone who is frantic and falling, holding on for dear life, trying to stay in control but unable to hang on for another moment. As we walk the high wire of the Christian life, we look at the end of our rope in a different way. No, the end is not that now we are better, stronger Christians who are more loving wives and mothers, more fruitful disciples, more faithful friends. In fact, the end is what we look forward to more than any of these things—although we are indeed striving for them in this life. Instead, the walk to the end is leading us to nothing less than being with God eternally in heaven itself.

If I fall off the wire every day, I must continue to walk with God's help, because I eagerly desire to reach the end. I strive for balance, not just so that I can be an expert funambulist, but because my walking gets me to heaven. If I live to the age of ninety, ready to die the next day, I might slip and fall. Even then, I will be compelled to climb back on that wire and take the journey all the way into God's loving arms. And the amazing thing is that I am so enveloped in the grace of God that when I do fall, it is as if I haven't fallen at all. God "credits" it to me as a perfect walk, simply because Jesus graciously gives me his righteousness.

Before I get to the end of my rope, I want my walk to make a difference in this world. I want to live a balanced life so that those around me can see the grace of God in me. Sometimes this striving for balance will make my life uncomfortable and challenging, but to know that the walk leads me, and others, to our heavenly Father makes it worth it.

Here I am on the high wire. I am walking, walking, growing stronger and more confident with each step. I have felt the woven strings of the net below numerous times, but I have also felt the hands of Jesus pulling me up, making me secure and urging me on. I am not thinking of the crowds, but I know they are sharing in my joy as I travel further along the rope (Hebrews 12:1). I am going to make it; I will not quit! God's grace has been too good to me for me to give up, and I will walk this wire for another year or for fifty more years. I will walk and walk and walk, until I reach the end. Only then will I look back, and I will say, "It was by the grace of God."

Group Session Eleven

Questions

1. After reading chapter 10, "Trust in God's Grace," write a description of your life before God's grace washed you clean.

2. If it had not been for the grace of God in your life, where might you be at this point?

3. Was it easier for you to accept God's grace when you first became a Christian? Why or why not?

4. How does God's grace train you to walk righteously through life?

Action Items

- Choose three passages about God's grace. Read them every day until your next group meeting.

- Write down what grace means to you personally.

Meeting Time

1. Share with each other your answers to each of the above questions and discuss.

2. What does Summer's statement (below) mean to you?

   He died for who I am, not for what I do.

3. Commit to read the epilogue, answer the questions, and do the action item before coming to the last meeting. Plan for that

meeting to be special—perhaps a dinner—to encourage one other and to celebrate the joys of seeking to live a balanced life. In short…have some fun together as you wrap up!

4. Pray together.

Remember that we are so enveloped in God's grace
that when we do fall, God "credits" it to us as a perfect
walk because of Jesus.

Epilogue

When I first received Tammy Fleming's chapter about how Jesus defines balance, I took a deep breath. She had written, "With the quest for balance in mind, what impresses me is the apparent lack of any of it in the life of our Lord." I thought, *Whoa. How can this be the pivotal chapter of a book on finding balance in our lives? People will read this chapter and give up their own quest for balance.*

I guess I had envisioned a nice little chapter on how balanced Jesus' life was and how we need to imitate him. Tammy's chapter tripped me up at first as the editor of this book. It caused me to wrestle with the whole question of balance and what it really does mean. And after all, this is what the book is all about: wrestling with the question and coming to a Biblical answer that we can implement in our lives.

After a while I realized that the key to what Tammy is saying comes a few paragraphs later where she points out that the problem is with our definition of balance—we try to apply our own humanistic definition to Jesus' life. She correctly identifies the truth that we want a simple formula that we can apply and then feel satisfied that we have accomplished "The Balanced Life." We want to do it ourselves: make our decisions, set our boundaries, plan our schedules, protect our time and so on. And certainly, we will need to do all these things, but just not first. First we must seek the kingdom of God and his righteousness; then he will help us with all these other details of living.

A Higher Call

As I worked with each of the subsequent chapters of this book, they (and their writers) called me higher. Though I realize that I will never have balance in my life apart from being rooted in the Scriptures, I can personally be tempted to lean on my own understanding (as Proverbs 3:5 says). When I do this, my yearning to imbibe the words of God wanes. And when that happens, I go into "tilt" mode in my walk without even realizing it. What a simple principle—to hold on to God's teaching—and yet how easily I can become complacent and distracted.

After many years of being a disciple of Jesus and knowing what is right to do in a myriad of life situations, I can begin to drift away from my focal point: Jesus himself. I can do the right thing, but not have the right heart—nothing is more unbalanced than this approach to life. When my focus is off, my whole outlook on life is skewed. Through working with this book, my conviction deepened: I will focus on Jesus and get my perspective from him. I will never give up this pursuit.

Winds have blown into my life. Winds that were uninvited and unwelcomed, yet they came all the same, threatening to batter my faith and leave it destroyed in their wake. Many women mentioned in this book are examples to me as my husband and I face the wearying wind of his multiple sclerosis. With God's continued help and grace, we will keep our focus and walk on...to the very end of the rope...holding on to God and to each other. And daily being grateful for liberal outpourings of God's extravagant grace.

I am grateful that I do not have to live in fear of falling off the high wire of life. God puts me on the wire, walks with me, picks me up when I fall, forgets about my fall, calls me righteous though I am not...and brings me home to live with him. He forgives my pride, my self-right-eousness and my self-reliance as long as I keep walking and keep repenting and keep trusting.

One Step at a Time

> One step at a time, dear Savior:
> I cannot take any more;
> The flesh is so weak and helpless:
> I know not what is before.
>
> One step at a time, dear Savior:
> O guard my faltering feet!
> Keep hold of my hand, dear Savior,
> Till I my journey complete.
>
> One step at a time, dear Savior,
> Till faith grows stronger in Thee;
> One step at a time, dear Savior,
> Till hope grows stronger in me.[1]
>
> —T. J. Shelton

"One step at a time, dear Savior," I say as I seek to walk daily in his presence and his power. "Keep hold of my hand, dear Savior," I say as fear and sin and guilt threaten to throw me down, to keep me from winning the eternal prize at the end of my walk. I feel the wind threatening to topple me and realize how powerless I am to do it on my own. My talent, my knowledge, my spiritual longevity are useless in supporting my walk. Only faith in the One who has walked before will bring me to the end of my high-wire walk...one step at a time.

---

[1] This old hymn is a great theme song for us as we seek to live the balanced life.

৵৶

The purpose of this book is not to overwhelm us, to give us an extended to-do list, to prove how ineffective we are. The purpose is to drive us to envision the life Jesus wants us to lead, to help us walk in his footsteps and to realize how very much we need him—every day. Balance isn't organization. Balance isn't perfection. Balance isn't even excellent implementation of the principles discussed in the chapters of this book. Balance is a humble reliance upon a just and loving God. Then we are free to learn and grow and to be more and more effective, to become more organized so we can use our time in better and better ways, to accept God's grace and forgiveness as we move forward.

Rejoice with me that God is teaching us, training us and above all, that he is moment by moment forgiving us. Let us together make up our minds to keep taking one step at a time and to keep trusting our Savior.

For his glory,
Sheila Jones

Group Session Twelve

Questions

1. After reading the epilogue, look back at your description of what it means to live a balanced life in Group Session 1. Has that definition changed any since reading this book? If so, how?

2. How have you felt overwhelmed and/or encouraged while reading this book? Please explain.

3. Look back over the song in the epilogue. Read each part and think about the high-wire walk of your life. How do the lyrics apply to what you have learned?

Action Item

• Decide on one guiding principle you will take with you from having read this book and from having shared your life and your heart with the women in your group.

Meeting Time

1. Share with each other your answers to each of the above questions and discuss.

2. Give each other feedback, particularly on question 2.

3. Take time to share with each person in the group one word that describes an aspect of her character or something about her that you appreciate. Start with one person and have everyone share about her; then move to a second person, then to the rest of the group.

4. Pray together.

❧

Remember that God puts you on the wire, walks with you,
picks you up when you fall, forgets about your fall,
calls you righteous though you are not…and brings you home
to live with him.

Other Helps

1
Balance Groups

It is immeasurably helpful to be going after a goal with a team. I remember once being on a tennis team with other women. I really hadn't had that kind of team experience since high school, and I had forgotten the sense of unity and focus that it engenders. We were pulling for each other as we played our games. We were not just trying to win our own game. You see, every win contributed to the whole team winning.

If five women are individually going after goals, they will not build synergy. This is true even if they are going after a common goal with varied paths of approach to that goal. They might love each other; they might encourage each other; but they will not be able to work effectively with each other to help the team "win." And, most likely, they will inadvertently pull each other in different directions because of each person's emphasis-of-the-month.

Consider, for example, the following scenario:

- Mary buys a book about organizing her home using a brilliantly conceived index-card system. She goes out and buys all the materials needed and sets about organizing her approach to keeping her house (and life) in order.

- Sarah sees a new book advertised on the Internet that promises five weeks to a renewed energy level by doing a daily exercise routine. She makes an online purchase and is determined that she is going to whip her unruly cellulite into tight submission.

- Marcey is frustrated that she has not been having consistent daily times with God in his word and in prayer. It seems that quite often she is getting up late and running behind all day long. She buys a devotional book at a local bookstore to help her have meaningful quiet times in the morning.

- Roberta is off in another direction: she is reading every book she can find on setting proper boundaries in her life, learning when and where and why to say no.

- Nanci, on the other hand, wants to have a stronger marriage and a more satisfying relationship with her husband. She has borrowed a book that her ministry leader recommends for newly married women.

These books are all excellent, and the principles they expound are helpful and needed. But these women will not be able to be a focused support for each other. Take a peek at these women as they are interacting with each other during week number two:

- Mary wants Sarah to go out and buy some index cards and start organizing her house and her cleaning schedule.

- Sarah feels overwhelmed by what Mary is sharing with her because she is trying to stay focused on her new exercise routine. The muscles in her legs and abdomen are sore, making it hard to think about going out and doing anything...much less buying index cards.

- Mary doesn't feel very supported by Sarah, and Sarah thinks Mary should quit sitting and writing on index cards—especially in view of those extra pounds she has put on in the last few months. She should be doing the exercise routine with her and losing weight.

- Meanwhile, Marcey cannot see why these other two are so focused on growing in areas that are not totally spiritual. She questions whether they are having meaningful times with God, and shares with them both what she is learning from her devotional book. Though she genuinely wants to help her friends, she is allowing a little self-righteousness to seep through her guard.

- Roberta doesn't want any of them to give her one more thing to do. She has set her boundaries and is carefully guarding them—no index cards, no involved exercise routine. Yes, she wants great times with God, but she doesn't want to feel guilty that she is not excited about Marcey's new devotional book.

- Nanci knows she needs to focus on being a better wife, so she wants to talk with Mary, Sarah and Roberta about how they have all become such loving companions to their husbands. But for some reason, they are having problems focusing on her questions.

The Better Part?

We might look at all these women and say, "Marcey has chosen the better part." And we would be right if we mean that time with God in prayer and study of the Bible must be at the core of our lives and at the center of our balance. Several chapters in the book make that very clear to us. But then, the other areas that the women want to grow in are also valid and Biblical goals. What we want to do with this book is to allow Mary, Sarah, Marcey, Roberta and Nanci to pull together and help each other find balance in their lives. They will all begin with strengthening their daily relationship with God. Then they will take other requisite steps together, helping each other balance as they go.

A good visual would be the Seven-Person Pyramid performed by the famous wire-walking Wallenda family. Arranged in three tiers, with four on the bottom, two in the middle and one on the top (standing on a chair!), all seven moved forward across the high wire as one. Each person's balance is synchronized with that of the others. Their need for each other is no illusion, as is their amazing feat.

Balance Groups

The book is formatted to be used in a small group setting. In order to evaluate our lives and to make new commitments to achieving balance, it is invaluable for other women to give us support, correction, encouragement and feedback. The members of these "Balance Groups" will be each other's trainers, mentors and cheerleaders as they work on the same things at the same time.

Certainly you can read and apply this book outside of a group setting, but we, the editor and authors, encourage you to pull in at least one woman who will attempt this walk with you.

I offer the following suggestions on how to best use this book in a group setting:

1. Read the chapter.
2. Put the action item(s) into practice for two weeks.
3. Meet with your group.
4. Discuss questions from the current Group Session questions.
5. Share progress.
6. Get input.

7. Give input.

8. Pray together.

Then, of course, read the next chapter and meet with the group two weeks later. The two helpful parts of this approach are

1. You are only taking one step at a time

2. You are walking with others, taking the same step

Group Session Questions

The questions for the group sessions follow each chapter. The members should read the preface and answer the questions for Group Session 1 before coming to the first meeting of the group. Then in your first session, you will make a commitment to help each other to put the principles of the book into practice.

The New Testament is full of passages explaining how we as disciples of Jesus are to be in each other's lives: encouraging, helping, correcting, loving, praying for, etc. These groups will be a forum in which these scriptures can be lived out...to God's glory.

—Sheila Jones

2
Order in Your Home

Our God is an ordered God, and he calls us to imitate his character. In our fast-paced society we can allow ourselves to become accustomed to disorder in our lives and in our homes. We excuse ourselves by saying, "I am just too busy to keep things neat." But, if we decide that order is a priority, can't we find the time to train our character to clean as we go and keep clutter in its place?

The two women who wrote the following reprinted articles would answer a resounding yes to this question. They will help you not only to desire order, but to do a better job of maintaining it.[1]

Ordered, but Not Obsessive

Helen Wooten
Los Angeles, USA

After each step of the creation process, "God saw that it was good." As he created order from the formless and empty earth, he was pleased. Throughout the first chapter of Genesis we can see God's plan emerge. We see how he put things together, making each part work beautifully with all the other parts.

---

1 Reprinted from the first edition (hardback) of *The Fine Art of Hospitality* (Billerica, Mass.: Discipleship Publications International, 1995), which is currently out of print.

As we create the foundation of our homes, we put into that house the order that reflects the nature of God—the same kind of order we see in the petals of flowers, in the feathers of birds, and in the consistency of the sunrise. The challenge for us is to reflect that same penchant for detail and order in our houses.

Another great example of God's order can be found in his instructions to the children of Israel as they were wandering in the wilderness. Exodus 25–27 records his plan for the building of the tabernacle. Every aspect of the building was exact and precise. No facet of this great undertaking was overlooked or considered unimportant. Then in Numbers 2 God gives specific instructions about the arrangement of the different tribes as they camped together. In Numbers 4 he gives instructions to the different Levite clans for moving the tabernacle from place to place. Each person had his particular task. Every time the Israelites pulled up camp, each Levite knew exactly what his responsibility was, exactly what he needed to carry to the new location. They weren't grabbing curtains and altars and scrambling to take the tent down. Even to the detail of carrying the tent pegs, they had their specific assignments.

Let's also look at God's ordered plan for the coming of Jesus. He began way back in Abraham's day (around 2000 BC), giving him the promise that he would bless the whole world through his seed. Then through the prophets Isaiah, Daniel, Joel and others, he predicted specifics about the coming of the Messiah. God kept following his plan through the birth and life of Jesus, and all the prophecies culminated at the resurrection. Because it is God's nature to stay with his plan, we thankfully now have salvation!

Order in Our Homes

As we look at these examples of order from the Scriptures, we see that if we are to have order in our lives and in our houses, we must also have a plan. Even though many of us today work outside of our homes, proper planning can enable us to accomplish efficiently whatever needs to be done at home. Just as every office has its ordered way to get things done, so should every home.

Of course, even with the best efforts, things do not always go according to our plans. Children get sick, parents get sick, or something comes up that needs immediate attention. All these things can distract us, but if we have a plan, we have something to go back to which will get us back on track.

For the most part, setting up specific things to do on specific days seems to be the best way to get started. This way we commit ourselves to accomplishing at least one or two tasks each day. For example, on Monday there always seems to be a lot of laundry after the weekend, so the laundry can be washed, folded and ironed, if needed, and clothes put away. The house usually needs a rather major cleaning each week, especially if there are children, so that could be the focus on another day. Grocery shopping could be accomplished on yet another day. For some people, making a daily list of things to be accomplished is a help. Beware: too long of a list can be overwhelming and too short of a list can be limiting.

Of course with any plan there needs to be flexibility, but not so much flexibility that work is not accomplished or that we make excuses about the lack of order in our homes. On the other hand, if we are too rigid, we can easily sin against our friends and family or anyone else who "interferes" with our routine. It is very important to have a joyful balance and to make sure that lack of order is not the norm. If we err in either direction, maintaining our homes becomes a burden, and we become grumblers and complainers, unable to rejoice in our responsibilities.

My Personal Plan Through the Years

When our five children were little, keeping the house neat and orderly was a challenge. Each evening after they were all in bed, I picked up anything out of place, cleaned the bathroom (after all those bedtime baths!), and only then would I sit down. Had I been a disciple of Jesus then, planning would have been even more crucial, as it is for disciples with families today. With very busy ministry schedules, our houses could look like children's playrooms much of the time if we are not consistent.

Taking time to think through my meals for the week helped me to write out a very specific grocery-shopping list. Therefore, I usually only went to the grocery store (with all my children) once a week. This helped not only in stress management, but in budget management as well.

I also needed a plan to keep the kitchen clean. I washed dishes as soon as dinner was over. When I got a dishwasher, I rinsed dishes and immediately put them into the dishwasher, washing the pots and pans and putting everything away in the cabinets. Now this is sometimes hard to do because of a group or one-on-one Bible study scheduled right after dinner. But the good thing about having a plan is that I can return to it before going to bed. That way I can start the day with a clean kitchen.

Character Development

To take advantage of every opportunity, we must have two definite aspects of character: (1) a trained eye to see the chaos and (2) a mindset that wants order in the home. Since I was trained by my mother in both of these areas, the only really difficult part for me was to do it and not to be lazy and indifferent. Becoming pregnant within the first year of our marriage, I discovered how quickly I could become self-indulgent and lazy. Morning sickness became my excuse not to get up. The excuse extended into the evening mealtime, so no dinner was prepared. For a while the sickness was legitimate, but as I look back, I know I should have held myself to some degree of order and productivity.

When I was growing up, my parents held me accountable; they taught and expected me to push through until the work was done...then I could rest. Isn't that God's way? He worked six days and rested on the seventh. Fortunately, as disciples, we have people in our lives to correct us if we are becoming lazy and to encourage us to push through and get our work done. It is then that rest is truly rewarding.

Be Open to Discipling

As disciples, even after learning how ordered God is and how we are to reflect his nature to others, we can rebel and be indifferent in the way we manage our homes. We may even have people in our lives giving us input and advice, but we consider it unimportant or intrusive. Some of us can think that those who disciple us are being too picky about unimportant details. But if this is the case, we need to go back and read Exodus 25–27 and Numbers 2 and 4 to see just how detailed God was in his instructions to the Israelites. And if we just do not seem to be able to get it together, we should keep asking for help. God will bless a heart that is willing, open and wants to learn.

Order is important to God; therefore, it must be important to us. There are many ways to get the work done, and it is up to us to find the best way, always being mindful that everything we do in our lives is to bring glory to God and to his kingdom.

Consistent, but Not Compulsive

Geri Laing
Raleigh/Durham, USA

God is "the same yesterday, today and forever" (Hebrews 13:8). Everything God is and does demonstrates his constancy and consistency—the flow of the seasons year after year, the coming of every new day, the utter reliability of his promises. God is always there, always working for our good, always working to sustain and maintain this world in which we live.

We are all greatly affected by our environment. Too many days of darkness and dreariness will depress even the most positive and cheerful among us. On the other hand, a bright, clear spring day lightens our steps and lifts our spirits! The same is true of the places we live. How do you feel when you arrive home only to be greeted by dirty dishes all over the counter and in the sink, piles of dirty laundry in every room, unmade beds and filthy bathrooms? I don't know about you, but just the thought of this scene makes me feel burdened and depressed.

We do not have to live like this, and in fact, disciples *must* not live like this! The real challenge, however, is not the great, inevitable clean-up; it is to keep it clean.

A Change of Mind and Heart

In my early years I certainly did not do much to imitate God in my personal surroundings. My unfortunate college roommate put up with a total slob, and even my husband, during our first years of marriage, must have been quite frustrated by my lack of order and neatness. Even an "eye for color" and some ability to decorate didn't do much good when it was surrounded by chaos! Of course, even in my most undisciplined, messy years, I did occasionally "clean up" and "clean out." But the order was short-lived because I didn't consistently live with order and discipline in my life.

As the years have gone by, however, I have become more convicted of God's desire for order and discipline. As God's child, everything in my life is a reflection of God himself. What a privilege and what an incredible challenge! My home is my little bit of creation, and the way I keep it speaks volumes about my view of God, of myself, and of my family and guests.

Most of us are able to at least straighten up our homes, apartments or rooms. Perhaps we do it under the duress of expected company, or maybe we have just reached the point of, "I can't stand this mess any longer!" The frustration comes because, once we have everything cleaned up, we cannot seem to keep it that way. The great challenge is to keep a home that is clean and neat while still allowing those who live there the freedom to do just that—*live!* We are a people of extremes: we either don't care enough about creating homes that are neat, clean and attractive or we are obsessed with the state of our surroundings, becoming selfish, greedy and unloving. God made a beautiful world and he keeps it that way. Why? So we can live in it and enjoy it. So should be the state of our personal surroundings, our homes.

I asked my children how they felt about having a clean house. They talked about how important it was for them to be able to bring their friends to a neat and attractive home. We tend to think children don't care about these things, but in fact, they do. Their friends have often commented that our home seemed so nice and "cleaned up." My children also went on to describe how they felt when they visited other people's homes that were messy or dirty. They all expressed embarrassment for their friends and their friends' families.

Once we are convinced that cleanliness and order should be maintained on a consistent, daily basis, what are some of the practical things we can do to bring this about?

Every Day

Make your bed first thing in the morning. It's amazing how much nicer a bedroom can look by just making the bed. It only takes a few minutes, but it is one of those things that is hard to get back to once the day begins.

When the children were young, I usually put only a fitted bottom sheet on their beds. Since each had a blanket they used at night, they only had to fold it and pull up a bedspread to make their beds. This was a part of their morning routine.

Keep the kitchen cleaned up and uncluttered. Get into the habit of cleaning up after every meal. Keep dishes washed and put away or rinsed and in a dishwasher whenever they are used, and teach your entire family to do the same. Teach everyone to clean "as they go," keeping crumbs and spills wiped and swept up. Does the microwave need cleaning or the stovetop wiping? Do these things when you notice them; it takes about thirty seconds when we do them as we go.

I keep only a few decorative things on my kitchen counters. Everything else has its own place. Have you ever really looked at the small appliances that are probably covering your counter space? Most of them are certainly not very attractive, they are quite bulky, and we really do not use them as often as we might think. The only appliance I leave out is my coffeemaker. Everything else I store in convenient, out-of-sight places: under counters or in drawers. This goes a long way toward making a kitchen look clean and in order.

Straighten up before you go to bed. Pick up the little odds and ends still lying around at the end of the day: children's toys, cast-off shoes and unhung jackets. There is nothing worse than greeting a fresh new day with clutter and confusion. It makes me feel burdened and overwhelmed before the day has really even begun.

Don't forget the dirty clothes. For those with small families, laundry may not be a tremendous burden and can be done once or twice a week. However, for those with larger families the laundry can be one of the most overwhelming tasks of the week. As soon as everything is finally washed, dried, folded and put away, several more loads appear out of nowhere. These suggestions may help:

- Teach everyone to bring their dirty clothes, sheets or towels to a laundry room or designated place at the end of the day.

- Start a load of wash first thing in the morning, and then sort out the next load.

- Folding clothes is a great job for older children, especially when they are sitting and watching television. Teach them to fold and put the clean clothes and laundry in the appropriate rooms.

Every Week

Get rid of the dust and dirt. Most houses need a good dusting once a week and a thorough vacuuming once or twice a week. Keep up with it and it's a breeze; let it go and it's miserable.

Clean those bathrooms! Bathrooms that are cleaned well once a week tend to stay clean and don't take nearly the time to clean as those that are only dealt with when the slime of mildew and the scum of neglect have begun to grow.

Again, teach everyone to clean and wipe up as they go: dirty clothes should be taken to the laundry basket, towels hung, toothbrushes and toothpaste put away, floors swept and counters wiped. As in the kitchen, organize so that very little is left out on the counters and everything has a specific storage place.

If you need help, get it. Maintaining a home is a challenge to the most disciplined among us. Keeping a clean home seems next to impossible for mothers who juggle both families and jobs. Professional help every week or two for those who can afford it can take pressure off a busy family. And even though a professional cleaning service is not in many of our budgets, there is still a way to get help. I have often hired an older high school student or a college student to clean for two or three hours each week. It takes a load off of me to have my bathrooms thoroughly cleaned and my house dusted. If she has time, she may run the vacuum cleaner. When those things are done, I can keep up with the rest fairly comfortably. I pay her more than she can make baby-sitting or even at a minimum-wage job, so it's worth it for her, and yet I still pay less than I would pay a cleaning service.

Every So Often

Get rid of the things you don't need and use. Several years ago when we moved to North Carolina, we had to store most of our belongings while we lived temporarily in a small apartment. "Temporary" turned out to be nearly a year. Some of the stored things we really needed and missed, but I was truly amazed at how many things we never missed at all. When we finally did move into our home, I didn't want to crowd it with all the "things" we didn't need. We had several garage sales, sold items in the newspaper, gave things away, and finally just threw away large amounts of clutter. My rule of thumb is: if you haven't used it, worn it, or looked at it for close to a year, toss it. You'll never miss it!

It is uncanny; we can regularly pare down our possessions, but they always seem to "grow back." Several times a year, I go through closets and cabinets searching for what is outgrown, never used, worn-out or broken. My children and husband have sometimes thought me to be a bit heartless as I threw away rubber-band balls, torn-up T-shirts, two-year-old schoolwork, paper-clip chains, fossilized Halloween candy, and various other sentimental items, but even God declares that "there is a time to keep and a time to throw away"! (Ecclesiastes 3:6)

Everyone Helps

As I have often told my children, "We all live here, we all make the mess, so we all clean it up." It is amazing how much easier it is to maintain a home when everyone helps. Children can do much more than we often expect of them, and it is important for them to learn to be responsible and to do things well. From a young age children can be taught where toys belong and be expected to put them there. Older children can do many things, from keeping their own rooms clean and straightened, to doing the dishes and cleaning up the kitchen, folding clothes, dusting and vacuuming. (Just remember that they are not slaves or indentured servants, but rather, loved and cherished members of a family!)

Put these things into practice and watch as chaos begins to subside, laughter is restored, and even your blood pressure returns to normal. As you begin to enjoy the results of these changes, however, be careful that the pendulum does not swing too far in the *other* direction. Just as I once was irresponsible and undisciplined, which was reflected in my surroundings, I now struggle with a different problem: I sometimes care *too* much about our home's appearance. God's world reflects his heart of love, and my home also expresses my heart. I therefore want it to be a testament of my love and care for people, rather than a mirror of frustration and impatience. Unfortunately, developing this balance is much easier said than done.

There are a few things that I have had to accept and continually remember about the work of running a home and a household:

1. It will never be all done.

2. It will never be perfect.

3. It will never stay that way.

Accept these facts, and it will be so much easier to relax and enjoy life!

Our homes are for living and living is for people. We must not ever forget this. One day our children will be grown and gone. Yes, they will remember and appreciate all the ways we physically took care of them and met their needs (probably more than they do now). But above all, they will remember and cherish the things we did together in our homes: the laughter, the hugs, the jokes, the good times. They will remember the family times more than the family room, the bedtime talks and stories more than the bedroom, and the mealtimes together more than the meals themselves. The same is true of all those who will have come through our homes. The love and joy they experienced there will be remembered long after the messes are cleaned up and order is restored. If I could add a verse on to 1 Corinthians 13, God's chapter on love, it would be: "If I am able to clean my house until it shines and polish it until it sparkles, but have not love, it is no more than an empty shell and is worth nothing!"

Let us therefore imitate our awesome Creator and loving Father by reflecting in our own tiny pieces of creation the love, compassion and beauty he has lavished upon us.

Editor's Note: Sandra Felton's fun and practical book *The New Messies Manual: The Procrastinator's Guide to Good Housekeeping* (Grand Rapids: Fleming H. Revell, 2001) is an excellent resource to help "messies" bring order to their homes. Also check out her Web site at www.messies.com.

Decluttering Your Home

Various books on organizing your home give similar advice about how to get started. Consider the following method, and happy cleaning!

- Get four medium sized boxes.
- Give them the following labels:

  Throw Away

  Give Away

  Store

  Relocate

- Start at your front door and work clockwise, tackling whatever closet, corner, shelf or bureau you come to.
- Go through whatever is there and put items in each of the boxes as needed.
- When you stop, either deal with the material already collected, or wait until the boxes are full after another attack or two.
- Work steadily throughout the next few weeks as you have time.
- Leave out only what is useful and what encourages you. Show clutter no mercy.

Contributors

Linda Brumley serves as a women's ministry leader in the Seattle Church of Christ. Her husband, Ron, is an elder with the church, and they also oversee the children's ministry. The Brumleys have four married children. Linda is co-editor of *She Shall Be Called Woman, Volumes 1 and 2,* anthologies on women of the Bible published by DPI. She is also a contributing author for *The Fine Art of Hospitality* and *Life and Godliness for Everywoman, Volumes 1 and 2.* Linda's favorite hobby is being a grandmother to "ten of the greatest kids in the world."

ထ

Kitty Chiles became a disciple of Jesus in 1990 in Tallahassee, Florida. She is a vice president of HOPE *worldwide*, overseeing the programs in the ACES (Africa, Caribbean, Empire States and Southeast US) sector, along with her husband, Bud. Prior to working for HOPE *worldwide,* Kitty was co-owner and vice president of Chiles Communications, Inc., a governmental relations firm in Florida. She was a member of the Florida council to raise funds to restore Ellis Island and served as a board member of Florida House, the state's Washington Embassy. She is a contributing author in *A Profession of Faith, Volume 1,* an anthology published by DPI. She and Bud have been married for more than twenty-five years and have three children.

ထ

Tammy Fleming and her husband, Andy, planted the Moscow Church of Christ and provided leadership that led to churches being planted throughout the former Soviet Union. She is a women's ministry leader, and works with her husband to oversee the churches in the Middle East sector of the International Churches of Christ. She also helps her husband as he oversees the administration of the churches worldwide. Tammy is a contributing author for *A Man in All Seasons, Volume 1* and *She Shall Be Called Woman, Volume 2,* anthologies published by DPI. Tammy is a gifted songwriter and singer. She and Andy are the parents of two children.

❧

Terrie Fontenot and her husband, Mike, lead the Hampton Roads Church of Christ in Virginia. She is the women's ministry leader and Mike is the lead evangelist and an elder. The Fontenots began and then led a church in Sydney, Australia, for thirteen years. They continue to give direction and oversight to the Australian family of churches and other churches in the British Commonwealth sector of the International Churches of Christ. They have three grown daughters and one son-in-law. Terrie enjoys riding her bicycle, crocheting, playing tennis and hanging out with her dog, Barney. She is a contributing author for *She Shall Be Called Woman, Volume 1* and *Glory in the Church,* anthologies published by DPI.

❧

Sally Hooper is a women's ministry leader in the Dallas-Fort Worth Church of Christ, where her husband serves as an elder. They currently lead the spiritual recovery ministry, which is focused on encouraging the faith of those going through challenging times. She is a contributing author for *The Fine Art of Hospitality* and *She Shall Be Called Woman, Volume 1,* anthologies published by DPI. Sally and Bill have three married children and five grandchildren. She enjoys wallpapering, reading about and visiting other countries, and experimenting with low-fat recipes.

❧

Kay S. McKean is the women's ministry leader of the Boston Church of Christ where her husband, Randy, is the lead evangelist. Together they lead the New England-Continental Europe sector of the International Churches of Christ. She and Randy have started churches in several countries. Kay is the author of *Our Beginning: Genesis Through the Eyes of a Woman* and co-author of *Love Your Husband*. She is also a contributing author for several anthologies published by DPI, including *The Fine Art of Hospitality; She Shall Be Called Woman, Volumes 1 and 2;* and *Life and Godliness for Everywoman, Volumes 1 and 2.* Randy and Kay have two children and one son-in-law. Kay enjoys reading, sitting in the sunshine and walking her Shetland sheepdog named Lance.

❧

Shelley Metten has been married thirty-two years to her husband, Greg, a veterinarian. After becoming Christians in San Diego in 1980, they served as missionaries in India for five years and in Tokyo for three years. Shelley has a master's degree in physiology and a PhD in anatomy. She has served on the faculty at San Diego State University, Harvard Medical School, Tokai Medical School (Tokyo, Japan) and UCLA Medical School, where she is currently an associate professor of medicine. She is a contributing author for *The Fine Art of Hospitality; She Shall Be Called Woman, Volume 1;* and *A Profession of Faith, Volume 1.* Shelley and Greg have two married children.

ॐ

Barbara Porter is a graduate of Harvard Law School who has decided to use her persuasive abilities to bring others to Christ. She and her husband, John, lead the Saō Paulo Church of Christ in Brazil. They also have the oversight responsibility of the churches of the International Churches of Christ in the southern part of South America. She is a contributing author for *She Shall Be Called Woman, Volume 2* and *The Promises of God,* anthologies published by DPI. Barbara enjoys music and working with theatrical productions. She and John have two children.

ॐ

Kim Sapp is the women's ministry leader of the Atlanta Church of Christ where her husband, Steve, is the lead evangelist. Together they oversee the churches of the International Churches of Christ in North Carolina, South Carolina and Georgia. Several years ago Kim enjoyed leading aerobics classes for the international athletes during the Atlanta Olympics. Currently she swims for exercise and loves to read—especially fiction. She is a contributing author for *She Shall Be Called Woman, Volume 2,* an anthology on women of the Bible published by DPI. Kim and Steve have three children.

ॐ

Sheila Jones is Associate Editor of Discipleship Publications International. She is married to Tom Jones, former Editor in Chief of DPI and an elder in the Northwest region of the Boston Church of Christ. She is the author of *9 to 5 and Spiritually Alive,* coauthor of *To Live Is Christ,* and editor of several anthologies including *The Fine Art of Hospitality; She Shall Be Called Woman, Volumes 1 and 2;* and *Life and Godliness for Everywoman, Volumes 1 and 2.* She and her husband have three grown daughters and one son-in-law. They also have a black and white Shi Tzu named Lydie, seen below.

photo by Gordon Ferguson